# 20TH CENTURY AMERICAN SHORT STORIES
## REVISED EDITION
## VOLUME 1

## Jean A. McConochie
### Pace University, New York

**Heinle & Heinle Publishers**
I(T)P An International Thomson Publishing Company

Pacific Grove • Albany • Bonn • Boston • Cincinnati • Detroit • London • Madrid • Melbourne • Mexico City
New York • Paris • San Francisco • Tokyo • Toronto • Washington

Heinle & Heinle Publishers
20 Park Plaza
Boston, MA 02116 U.S.A.

International Thomson
    Publishing
Berkshire House 168–173
High Holborn
London WC1V7AA
England

Thomas Nelson Australia
102 Dodds Street
South Melbourne, 3205
Victoria, Australia

Nelson Canada
1120 Birchmont Road
Scarborough, Ontario
Canada M1K5G4

International Thomson
    Publishing Gmbh
Königwinterer Strasse 418
53227 Bonn
Germany

International Thomson
    Publishing Asia
Block 211 Henderson Road
    #08–03
Henderson Industrial Park
Singapore 0315

International Thomson
    Publishing—Japan
Hirakawacho-cho Kyowa
    Building, 3F
2-2-1 Hirakawacho-cho
Chiyoda-ku, 102 Tokyo
Japan

The publication of *Twentieth Century American Short Stories,* Volume I was directed by the members of the Newbury House Publishing Team at Heinle & Heinle:

Erik Gundersen, Editorial Director
John F. McHugh, Market Development Director
Kristin Thalheimer, Production Services
    Coordinator
Elizabeth Holthaus, Director of Production and Team
    Leader
Amy Lawler, Managing Developmental Editor

Also participating in the publication of this program:

Publisher: Stanley J. Galek
Project Manager: Margaret Cleveland
Assistant Editor: Karen P. Hazar
Associate Production Editor: Maryellen Eschmann
Manufacturing Coordinator: Mary Beth Hennebury
Interior Designer: Winston • Ford Design
Compositor: Pre-Press Company, Inc.
Cover and interior photos: Jon Nickson
Cover Designer: Kim Wedlake

**Library of Congress Cataloging–in–Publication Data**

A collection of twentieth century American short stories Volume 1/[compiled
    by] Jean A. McConochie.
        p.   cm.
    ISBN 0–8384–6146–8
    1. English language—Textbooks for foreign speakers. 2. United
States—Social life and customs—20th century—Fiction. 3. Short
stories, American. 4. Readers.   I. McConochie, Jean A.
PE1128.A56  1994
813' .010805—dc20                                                    94–43027
                                                                          CIP

Heinle & Heinle Publishers is a division of International
Thomson Publishing, Inc.

Manufactured in the United States of America.

ISBN 0-8384-4850-X

10  9  8  7  6  5  4  3  2  1

*For my mother,*
*Marian Brenckle McConochie,*
*who introduced me to the enchantment of literature*

# Contents

## Introduction

# Contents

# Introduction

*Twentieth Century American Short Stories*, Volume 1, is one of three related publications designed to introduce English-as-a-second or foreign language students to the richness and variety of modern American short fiction. The complete program includes:

- *Twentieth Century American Short Stories*, Volume 1 — high intermediate

- *Twentieth Century American Short Sories*, Volume 2 — advanced

- *Twentieth Century American Short Stories*, An Anthology — a collection of all of the stories from Volumes 1 and 2, without the activities

## How THE STORIES HAVE BEEN CHOSEN

While the choices necessarily reflect the editor's tastes, the selections are intended to suggest the cultural and ethnic diversity of twentieth-century American fiction. Some of the stories in this book are humorous; others are serious. Some are set in large cities—New York, Chicago, Los Angeles; others take place in suburban or rural areas of New England, the South, the Midwest, or the West. Together, the stories explore universal questions of relations within families and between the sexes, changing customs and traditions, and conflicts of culture that aren't always recognized by those involved. All are superb tales that can be read again and again with increasing pleasure.

All of the stories are relatively short, ranging in length from approximately five hundred to approximately six thousand words. They are appropriate in content and vocabulary for high-intermediate (Volume 1) or advanced (Volume 2) students of English as a second or foreign language. The stories are also suitable for high school or college students whose first language is English, though they would probably find the "Uncommon Words or Meanings" section unnecessary.

The selections are from all but the first two decades of the twentieth century, with half of the stories in Volume 1 and three-quarters of those in Volume 2 published after mid-century. All of the twenty-four stories represent an American point of view, though two stories are set outside the United States, two are by British authors who place their stories in an American context, and five of the twenty-four authors spoke another language before they learned English. While many of the stories have been translated into other languages, all of them were originally written in English.

## HOW THIS EDITION DIFFERS FROM THE FIRST EDITION

Of the nine stories in the first edition, five have been kept for Volume 1: "The Unicorn in the Garden" by James Thurber, "The Chaser" by John Collier, "Love" by Jesse Stuart, "The Use of Force" by William Carlos Williams, and "The Lottery" by Shirley Jackson. "The Orphaned Swimming Pool" by John Updike appears in Volume 2, as does Ernest Hemingway's "Hills Like White Elephants," which has been substituted for his story "The Killers."

For each author, the biographical material has been expanded and now forms part of the introduction to the story. The glossary now precedes the story, with no interruption of the text to indicate glossed words, and with objective criteria for choosing words to be glossed. Grammar and vocabulary exercises have been replaced by questions concerned with style and with connections between and among stories.

## HOW THE VOLUMES ARE ORGANIZED

The stories in Volume 1 are, on average, slightly shorter and simpler in structure and vocabulary than those in Volume 2. Within each volume, the stories have been ordered by increasing complexity of plot and vocabulary, with an eye to balance in content, tone, and style. However, while there is some cross-referencing in the "Making Connections" questions, the stories otherwise function as self-contained units.

The **Introduction** to each story presents the author in the context of his or her time and previews the story. Where appropriate, it also includes suggestions for further reading.

**Unusual Words or Meanings** provides brief explanations of words that can't easily be found in a dictionary: cultural references (such as brand and place names), idioms, slang, words in languages other than English, and words used in a meaning other than the most common (here defined as the first meaning listed in the *Oxford Advanced Learner's Dictionary*, Third Edition). Words are defined only as they are used in the story and are presented in the order in which they appear in the story. Nouns are glossed in their singular form, preceded by *a* or *an* if the noun is countable, and time-oriented verbs are glossed in their *to* (infinitive) form.

Each **story** is presented as the author wrote it: nothing has been simplified; any extra space between paragraphs was put there by the author; the presence or absence of quotation marks for direct speech is the author's choice. While words glossed in the "Unusual Words or Meanings" section are not marked in the text, line numbers have been added in the margin to facilitate discussion. Following the convention of many literature texts, the original publication date appears in square brackets at the end of the story.

**Understanding the Story** questions, rather than asking for simple facts, require synthesis and analysis. Their purpose is to direct readers back to the story, encouraging careful reading. This and the following sections also provide an opportunity for students to explore the uses of several literary terms that are commonly used by college-educated speakers of English, including *allusion, connotation, foreshadowing, irony, metaphor, personification, simile,* and *stereotype.* The literary terms are briefly defined the first time they are used in a chapter, with the aim of helping readers to become comfortable with the terms and how they are used.

**Developing a Way with Words** offers a closer look at a stylistic aspect of the story, examining sentences that share a common element or exploring questions of vocabulary usage.

**Making Connections** provides a wide range of options for discussion, with most of the topics also being suitable as points of departure for writing. Readers may be invited to speculate on the characters, to dramatize the story, to explore a related story or poem, to write a letter, to analyze some aspect of plot or imagery, to compare and contrast the story with one previously read in class, or to connect the story with events in their own lives. The topics are at varying levels of complexity, so that teachers and students in a particular class may choose the one or two topics best suited to their needs. If there is a film or video version of the story, information on it forms the basis for the last question of this section.

If readers want to read more when they have finished these stories, the books' purpose will have been achieved.

## ACKNOWLEDGEMENTS

Many friends and colleagues have helped to make this book a reality. Indeed, the collaborative aspect was the greatest pleasure in preparing the manuscript. It is now my honor to name those who have contributed their talents and supportive concern to the project.

David R. Werner provided superb coaching at every stage of writing and production; his intelligence, understanding, and sense of humor have enriched the book. All in all, Dave and the boys kept both me and Mike (my computer) running smoothly throughout the process. My thanks for it all.

Winifred A. Falcon, Karla Jay, Laurie Lafferty, Jaime Mantilla, and Brett Sherman, as well as Heinle & Heinle readers, all helped in shaping the final selection of stories. Anne McCormick offered invaluable support in pursuing permissions, which are gratefully acknowledged at the back of the book. In addition, the authors Mari Evans, Mark Steven Hess, Lucy Honig, Judy Troy, W. D. Wetherell, and Hisaye Yamamoto responded graciously and generously to the queries of a stranger. My thanks to them, and indeed to all the writers whose stories and poems have provided me with such intense pleasure over the past two years.

Laurie Lafferty and Dave Werner patiently read successive drafts; their creative criticism and perceptive comments strengthened every chapter. One or more chapters also benefitted from the insights of Winnie Falcon, Jaime Mantilla, and Pat Rigg, as well as my editor Amy Lawler, and the following reviewers commissioned by Heinle & Heinle:

Lynne Barsky, *Suffolk Community College, New York*
Meggie Courtright, *University of Illinois, Urbana-Champaign*
Kay Ferrell, *Rancho Santiago Community College, California*
Judith Garcia, *Miami-Dade Community College*
Thomas Hardy, *University of Southern Mississippi*
Virginia Herringer, *Pasadena City College*
Joe McVeigh, *University of Southern California*
Melissa Munroe, *Boston University*
Karen Richelli-Kolbert, *Manhattanville College*
Ross Savage, *North Hennepin Community College,
    Minnesota*
Diane Starke, *El Paso Community College*
Mark Stepner, *Boston University*
Mo-Shuet Tam, *San Francisco Community College*

Additional field-testing was generously provided by Lise
Winer and her Southern Illinois University graduate students Lori
Brown, Tenley Chambliss, Randy Cotten, Simone DeVito, Laura
Halliday, Robert Lee, and Paula Tabor, who tried many of the sto-
ries out with their undergraduate students. My thanks to all.

For additional clarification of assorted points, I am indebted
to Judith Bauduy, Paul Cochran, Sergio Gaitán, Janet Ghattas,
John Lafferty, George Marino, Shirley Miller, Tina Pratt, Allan
Rabinowitz, Muriel Shine, Tippy Schwabe, and Patricia and Sid-
ney Wittenberg, as well as to Jane Knowles, reference librarian at
Radcliffe College. At Pace University's Henry Birnbaum Library, I
benefitted from the creative determination of reference librari-
ans Michelle Fanelli, and Tom Snyder and from the legacy of the
late Bruce Bergman, whose passion for acquisition has enriched
us all.

Also at Pace University, Sherman Raskin, chair, Department
of English, offered unstinting encouragement throughout the
manuscript preparation, and Charles Masiello, dean, Dyson College of Arts and Sciences, kindly granted me a one-semester sab-
batical leave to complete the manuscript. My thanks to both of
them.

At Heinle & Heinle, Erik Gundersen proposed this revision
and expansion of the original text, Amy Lawler tactfully suggested editorial improvements, Kristin Thalheimer and Margaret
Cleveland meticulously supervised production, and Andreas Martin developed a creative marketing plan. I am grateful to all of

them for enabling me to benefit from their professional exper-
tise. For friendly and reliable technical support, Sanford Fox and
his crew at Foxy Copy were, as always, indispensible.

The initial impetus for this book came, many years ago, from
my colleague and friend Gary Gabriel, whom I thank once again.

# No Speak English

"I believe she is afraid to come out because she doesn't speak English."

# No Speak English

## Sandra Cisneros
## (born 1954)

In the last decade of the twentieth century, Sandra Cisneros has established herself as one of the important new voices in American literature. Cisneros, who now lives in San Antonio, Texas, was born and raised in Chicago. The daughter of a Mexican father and Mexican American mother, she grew up in a largely Spanish-speaking neighborhood and spent her childhood "being quiet," as was expected of a daughter in a Latino household and of a Latina girl in the society at large.*

Even in graduate school, Cisneros found that teachers paid little attention to women and that discussions excluded anyone who wasn't from a white middle-class family. When talking about the literary symbolism of houses, for example,  one teacher spoke of attics (the storage space under the roof) as symbols of a family's past. Cisneros' family had always lived in an apartment and, as she says, "the third floor front doesn't come with an attic." Gradually, however, she realized there were subjects on which she was the expert. When other students talked about cupolas (a tiny room with windows on four sides on the roof of a Victorian house), she thought about narrow wooden back porches (a common feature of older three-story apartment buildings in Chicago). When others talked of swans, she thought about rats. Whatever her

*These direct quotations are reconstructed from notes taken during Cisneros' plenary address at the twenty-seventh annual convention of Teachers of English to Speakers of Other Languages, Atlanta, Georgia, 1993.

classmates wrote about, she presented the opposite. Gradually, Cisneros found herself with a number of stories about growing up in a Mexican American community, stories that were valuable precisely because they weren't like anyone else's. Teaching high school dropouts in Chicago the next year, Cisneros gathered additional stories from her students. Soon she had a collection of forty-four, including "No Speak English." Several years later, they were published by Women of Color Press under the title *The House on Mango Street.*

Although Cisneros by then really wanted to be a writer, she took another teaching job to support herself. Trying to be "perfect" as a teacher brought her to near-suicidal despair, but she was rescued by a National Endowment for the Arts Fellowship. "It reminded me that I was a writer," Cisneros says, "and it gave me *attitude.*" This self-confidence was supported by critics' praise for *The House on Mango Street* when it was reissued by a major publisher in 1989. Since that time, she has published *Woman Hollering Creek and Other Stories* (1991), set mainly in San Antonio, and *My Wicked Wicked Ways* (1992), her first book of poetry.

The stories in *The House on Mango* Street are very short, some less than a page. All of them are narrated by fourteen-year-old Esperanza Cordero, a girl whose first name means "Hope." Some of the stories are about her and some are about her girlfriend Rachel; others, including "No Speak English," are about their neighbors. What do you suppose that title means? Who do you suppose says it?

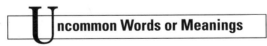

## Uncommon Words or Meanings

*Words or phrases from the story are explained if they are cultural references (including words in a language other than English), idioms, or slang, or if the meaning is not the first listed in a standard dictionary. The words or phrases appear in their order of first use in the story.*

**A note on translation:** The Spanish words in this story (marked in this list with a star) are explained according to their meaning in Mexican Spanish; the meaning or implications in other Spanish-language communities may be different.

**\*Mamacita** ("*Mamacita* is the big mama")—"little mother"; a term of endearment that shows both love and respect for the mother's authority.

**a big mama** ("Mamacita is the *big mama*")—(slang) a man's wife or lover, his "number one woman."

**\*Mamasota** ("her name ought to be *Mamasota*")—(vulgar slang) a woman with big buttocks or "a large rear end."

**mean** ("I think that's *mean*.")—deliberately unkind.

**a yellow taxi** ("arrived in a *yellow taxi*")—an officially licensed taxicab.

**fuchsia** ("*fuchsia* roses")—a deep purplish-red color.

**\*Poof!**—an interjection (sometimes spelled ¡Puf! or ¡Pfffs! ) roughly equivalent to "Ouf!"; said when a strenuous physical effort suddenly succeeds.

**lavender** ("her *lavender* hatboxes")—a pale purple color.

**Holy smokes**—(slang) an exclamation of surprise; some say "holy smoke."

**\*¿Cuándo?**—When?

**\*¡Ay, Caray!**—An exclamation of impatience, with the sense of "That doesn't make any difference! That's how it is."

**skinny** ("the only *skinny* thread")—very thin.

**tin** ("the language that sounds like *tin*")—a soft silver-white metal with a dull, flat sound.

# No Speak English

Mamacita is the big mama of the man across the street, third-floor front. Rachel says her name ought to be *Mamasota,* but I think that's mean.

The man saved his money to bring her here. He saved and
5    saved because she was alone with the baby boy in that country. He worked two jobs. He came home late and he left early. Every day.

Then one day Mamacita and the baby boy arrived in a yellow taxi. The taxi door opened like a waiter's arm. Out stepped
10   a tiny pink shoe, a foot soft as a rabbit's ear, then the thick ankle, a flutter of hips, fuchsia roses and green perfume. The man had to pull her, the taxi driver had to push. Push, pull. Push, pull. Poof!

All at once she bloomed. Huge, enormous, beautiful to
15   look at, from the salmon-pink feather on the tip of her hat down to the little rosebuds of her toes. I couldn't take my eyes off her tiny shoes.

Up, up, up the stairs she went with the baby boy in a blue blanket, the man carrying her suitcases, her lavender hatboxes,
20   a dozen boxes of satin high heels. Then we didn't see her.

Somebody said it's because she's too fat, somebody because of the three flights of stairs, but I believe she doesn't come out because she is afraid to speak English, and maybe this is so since she only knows eight words. She knows to say:
25   *He not here* for when the landlord comes. *No speak English* if anybody else comes, and *Holy smokes.* I don't know where she learned this, but I heard her say it one time and it surprised me.

My father says when he came to this country he ate hamandeggs for three months. Breakfast, lunch, and dinner. Haman-
30   deggs. That was the only word he knew. He doesn't eat hamandeggs anymore.

Whatever her reasons, whether she is fat, or can't climb the stairs, or is afraid of English, she won't come down. She sits all day by the window and plays the Spanish radio show and sings
35   all the homesick songs about her country in a voice that sounds like a seagull.

Home. Home. Home is a house in a photograph, a pink house, pink as hollyhocks with lots of startled light. The man paints the walls of the apartment pink, but it's not the same you know. She still sighs for her pink house, and then I think she cries. I would.

Sometimes the man gets disgusted. He starts screaming and you can hear it all the way down the street.

Ay, she says, she is sad.

Oh, he says, not again.

¿Cuándo, cuándo, cuándo? she asks.

¡Ay, Caray! We *are* home. This *is* home. Here I am and here I stay. Speak English. Speak English. Christ!

¡Ay! Mamacita, who does not belong, every once in a while lets out a cry, hysterical, high, as if he had torn the only skinny thread that kept her alive, the only road out to that country.

And then to break her heart forever, the baby boy who has begun to talk, starts to sing the Pepsi commercial he heard on T.V.

No speak English, she says to the child who is singing in the language that sounds like tin. No speak English, no speak English, and bubbles into tears. No, no, no as if she can't believe her ears.

[1989]

# Understanding the Story

*These questions call for analysis and synthesis of the story's main points.*

1. From the descriptions of Mamacita in the first six paragraphs of the story (lines 1–27), how do you picture her?

2. Like many new immigrants, Mamacita is having trouble adjusting to life in the United States.

   a. What three different suggestions are given for why Mamacita never leaves her apartment? Which suggestion seems most likely to you? Why?

   b. What does "No speak English" mean the first time it appears (line 25)? What does it mean in the final paragraph?

c. How well does Mamacita's eight-word vocabulary (lines 25–26) meet her needs? What other words might she need if she went outside? Why do you think the narrator, Esperanza, tells the story about "hamandeggs" (lines 28–31)?

3. Mamacita listens to Spanish music and sings Spanish songs about homesickness. Do you think these activities make her feel more or less homesick? When the man paints their apartment pink, why is that "not the same" (line 39)? Not the same as what?

4. What is the evidence that the man really wanted Mamacita to join him? How is his reaction to Chicago different from hers?

5. What question does the man hear in Mamacita's "¿Cuándo?" that makes him respond, "We *are* home. This *is* home" (line 47)? In what ways does Mamacita "not belong" (line 49)?

6. In the description "the only skinny thread that kept [Mamacita] alive, the only road out to that country" (lines 50–51), both "thread" and "road" are metaphors. That is, there is no real thread or road; the words "thread" and "road" mean something else and they present that meaning through an indirect or implied comparison.

   a. What do "thread" and "road" represent in terms of Mamacita's life? How are a thread and a road alike? What difference between them justifies using both words?

   b. What does the man do that makes Mamacita feel that he has "torn" that thread?

7. What is the final blow to Mamacita's hopes? How does she react to the blow? What does it mean to say that English is a "language that sounds like tin" (line 56)?

## Developing a Way with Words

*For those who wish to look more closely at how a story has been told, this section presents either distinctive features of the author's style or, for a few stories, a related literary text.*

1. Examine the following descriptions. The first four use *like* or *as* to make a direct comparison. (The literary term for that is a simile.) The other two are indirect—implied—comparisons. (The literary term for that is a metaphor, as in question 6 in the previous section.) Which of the five senses does each description evoke? Does it describe how something looks, how it sounds, how it feels, how it tastes, or how it smells?

   a. The taxi door opened like a waiter's arm. (line 9)

   b. a foot soft as a rabbit's ear (line 10)

   c. a voice that sounds like a seagull (lines 35–36)

   d. a pink house, pink as hollyhocks (lines 37–38)

   e. lots of startled light (line 38)

   f. bubbles into tears (line 57)

2. Write several descriptions of something that you can see from where you are sitting now. In two or three of the descriptions, use *like* or *as* in a direct comparison—a simile. In two or three, make an indirect or implied comparison—a metaphor. Try to use a different sense—sight, hearing, touch, taste, or smell—in each of your descriptions.

# Making Connections

*These options for discussion and writing (at varying levels of complexity) invite readers to connect the stories with their own experience and with other works of literature.*

1. What countries could "that country" (line 5) refer to? Would the story be stronger if Cisneros had specified a particular country? Why or why not?

2. How unusual is Mamacita's situation? Discuss that question, then write without stopping for ten minutes on one

of the following questions. After ten minutes, stop and discuss your answer with others in your class.

   a. What do you suppose Mamacita expected of life in Chicago?

   b. If you were in Mamacita's place, what would you do?

   c. If you were the man, what would you do?

   d. If you were Esperanza, would you try to help? Why or why not?

3. What do you imagine will happen to Mamacita and her family in the next two years? Write for ten minutes on what you think will become of her, the man, and their son. Then compare your answer with the answers of others in the class.

4. Have you had the experience of moving to a new place where you dressed differently from everyone else and didn't know much of the language? If so:

   a. What were the first words you learned? Did you make much progress? If so, how?

   b. Did your change your style of dress, or other obvious aspects of your life, to match those of the people around you? If so, what were some of the changes?

   c. How long did you stay? (Or are you still there?)

5. What sort of letters do you imagine the man and Mamacita wrote to each other after he left their country but before she came to Chicago? What sort of letters do you suppose Mamacita wrote from Chicago to her family at home? Write some of the letters, as you imagine them to have been.

6. Cisneros advises beginning writers, "Ask yourself what makes you different from anyone else—in your school, your neighborhood, your family." She also insists that "the things you can't talk about—the things that are so taboo that you can't even think about them—are what you have to write about." Following her advice, write two or three stories about your school, or neighborhood, or family when you were growing up.

# Popular Mechanics

"He reached
across the stove
and tightened his
hands on the
baby."

# Popular Mechanics

*Raymond Carver*
*(1938–1988)*

Raymond Carver identified himself as "a full-time member of the working poor." Born in Clatskanie, Oregon, Carver grew up thinking that, like his father, he would go to work in a lumber mill after high school. But six months in the mills was enough; he knew he wanted more. With his wife and their two young children, Carver moved to northern California, where he began college on a partial scholarship.

One of his teachers, the novelist John Gardner, helped Carver to revive his childhood interest in making up stories and encouraged him to find his own voice as a writer. Working nights at a succession of blue-collar jobs, Carver used the days to learn to write. Because the house was always noisy, he often worked in the family car. Because his writing time was limited, he concentrated on short pieces—a poem or story—that could be finished in one sitting. Carver also worked to strip the stories down to the bare minimum— "cutting them to the bone, and then cutting them a bit more," he joked. His first collection of stories—*Will You Please Be Quiet, Please* (1976)—led reviewers to speak of "Carver country," a fictional world in which working-class people struggle to make sense of their lives, or failing that, simply to get through them. But Carver had also been troubled by alcoholism, which finally led him to stop writing and destroyed his family life.

In 1977, realizing that he was drinking himself to death, Carver took his last drink and began what he later identified as his "second life." (He and his first wife separated that year and were divorced five years later.) Carver started writing again the following year, after meeting the poet Tess Gallagher. His next book, *What We Talk About When We Talk About Love* (1981), brought him world-wide recognition, with translations in more than twenty languages. His following collection, *Cathedral* (1983), marked a new direction in his work, with much longer stories that also carried a sense of hope. In 1988, Carver married Gallagher, was elected to the American Academy and Institute of Arts and Letters, and won two awards for his story "Errand," which is based on the death of the Russian writer Anton Chekov. However, he also suffered a relapse of lung cancer, for which he had been treated earlier, and died at home in Port Angeles, Washington, leaving five collections of short stories, five books of poetry, and one collection of prose and poetry.

"Popular Mechanics" first appeared in *What We Talk About When We Talk About Love* and was reprinted under the title "Little Things" in *Where I'm Calling From* (1988). Asked once about the sense of menace—of impending danger—in his stories, Carver said, "The people I've chosen to write about *do* feel menace, and I think many, if not most, people feel the world is a menacing place. . . . Try living on the other side of the tracks for a while. Menace is there, and it's palpable. "*The characters of "Popular Mechanics" certainly live on the wrong side of the tracks, in a three-room house heated only by a free-standing stove in the kitchen. For this young couple and their baby, what do you suppose the menace will prove to be?

* Larry McCaffrey and Sinda Gregory, "An Interview with Raymond Carver," reprinted in *Conversations with Raymond Carver*, edited by Marshall Bruce Gentry and William L. Stull (1990).

## Uncommon Words or Meanings

**Popular Mechanics** (title)—The name of a magazine dedicated to electronics, automobiles, wood-working projects, and other "manly" pursuits.

**slush** ("Cars *slushed* by")—partly melted snow; Carver has turned the noun into a verb.

**a scuffle** ("In the *scuffle*")—a rough, confused struggle or fight.

**a fist** ("Her *fisted* fingers")—a tightly closed hand, with the fingers turned under; Carver has turned the noun into an adjective.

Early that day the weather turned and the snow was melting into dirty water. Streaks of it ran down from the little shoulder-high window that faced the backyard. Cars slushed by on the street outside, where it was getting dark. But it was getting
5    dark on the inside too.

He was in the bedroom pushing clothes into a suitcase when she came to the door.

I'm glad you're leaving! I'm glad you're leaving! she said. Do you hear?

10    He kept on putting his things into the suitcase.

Son of a bitch! I'm so glad you're leaving! She began to cry. You can't even look me in the face, can you?

Then she noticed the baby's picture on the bed and picked it up.

15    He looked at her and she wiped her eyes and stared at him before turning and going back to the living room.

Bring that back, he said.

Just get your things and get out, she said.

He did not answer. He fastened the suitcase, put on his
20    coat, looked around the bedroom before turning off the light. Then he went out to the living room.

She stood in the doorway of the little kitchen, holding the baby.

I want the baby, he said.

25    Are you crazy?

No, but I want the baby. I'll get someone to come by for his things.

You're not touching this baby, she said.

The baby had begun to cry and she uncovered the blanket
30    from around his head.

Oh, oh, she said, looking at the baby.

He moved toward her.

For God's sake! she said. She took a step back into the kitchen.

35    I want the baby.

Get out of here!

She turned and tried to hold the baby over in a corner behind the stove.

But he came up. He reached across the stove and tightened
40　his hands on the baby.

Let go of him, he said.

Get away, get away! she cried.

The baby was red-faced and screaming. In the scuffle they knocked down a flowerpot that hung behind the stove.

45　He crowded her into the wall then, trying to break her grip. He held on to the baby and pushed with all his weight.

Let go of him, he said.

Don't, she said. You're hurting the baby, she said.

I'm not hurting the baby, he said.

50　The kitchen window gave no light. In the near-dark he worked on her fisted fingers with one hand and with the other hand he gripped the screaming baby up under an arm near the shoulder.

She felt her fingers being forced open. She felt the baby
55　going from her.

No! she screamed just as her hands came loose.

She would have it, this baby. She grabbed for the baby's other arm. She caught the baby around the wrist and leaned back.

60　But he would not let go. He felt the baby slipping out of his hands and he pulled back very hard.

In this manner, the issue was decided.

[1981]

## Understanding the Story

1. Who are "he" and "she"? Would the story be stronger if the characters had names? Why or why not?

2. How is the setting—the season, weather, time of day, and location—appropriate to the story? In what way has the weather "turned" (line 1)? How has the situation in the story turned?

3. Why do you think she is crying? What signs of emotion is he showing?

4. What do you think the baby represents to each of them? When do you suppose he got the idea of taking the baby with him? Is the baby a boy or a girl?

5. Do you think she is correct in saying that the man is hurting the baby (line 48)? Why or why not?

6. The last sentence of the story is deliberately ambiguous; that is, the author has intentionally left several possibilities for its meaning. What is "the issue"? In what "manner" is it decided? What are the various possibilities for answering those questions?

7. What do you think the title means? Why do you suppose Carver later changed the title to "Little Things"?

## D eveloping a Way with Words

1. In a story this "minimal," with so few words, any repetition carries great weight. Discuss the meaning—direct and indirect—of the references to light and darkness in the following sentences.

    a. Cars slushed by on the street **outside, where it was getting dark**. But it was **getting dark on the inside too**. (lines 4–5)

    b. He fastened the suitcase, put on his coat, looked around the bedroom before **turning off the light**. (lines 19–20)

    c. The kitchen **window gave no light. In the near-dark** he worked on her fisted fingers . . . . (lines 50–51)

2. Another aspect of Carver's stripped-down style is that there are almost no adjectives, so the ones that are used carry great weight. Find the seven adjectives (the first is "dirty" in line 2) and comment on their choice. How many adverbs are there?

3. Now look at the verbs.

    a. In the dialogue, almost everything is "he said, she said." Therefore, "she cried" (line 42) has great power. Where else does Carver use a verb to indicate tone of voice?

b. Which other verbs have special power because they are unusual? ("Slushed," line 3, is one example.)

c. For the most part, the reader is left to imagine the emotion behind the words. What do you think is the tone of the woman's words in the sentence "Oh, oh, she said, looking at the baby" (line 31)? Choose several other statements and discuss the emotion behind them and their possible tone.

## M aking Connections

1. Carver's story is reminiscent of two legendary stories about dividing a child between two women when each of the women claims to be the mother. Perhaps you will recognize one or both of them. Read the stories aloud, then discuss the questions following them.

## The Judgment of Solomon

*This story is from the Bible, the First Book of Kings, chapter 3, verses 16–27. The story has been retold to simplify the language.*

When God offered King Solomon any gift he wanted, Solomon asked for wisdom. He soon had a chance to test his gift, for two prostitutes came to him for a judgment.

5     The women had two babies with them, one alive and one dead. "We live in the same house, your majesty," the first woman said. "I recently had a baby and three days later this other woman also gave birth. But she accidentally rolled over her child during the night and it died. Then she got up and took my baby and left me with her dead child."

10     The second woman said, "No, the living child is mine and the dead one is hers. She is trying to take my child away from me."

King Solomon thought for a moment, then he called a
guard to come forward with a sword. "Cut the living child in
15 two," he said, "and gave half to each woman."

"No, no," cried the second woman. "Don't harm the child.
Give it to her."

"Not at all," snapped the first woman. "Divide the child so
that neither one of us has it."

20 Then Solomon said, "Give the child to the second woman,
for she is the true mother." And the people knew that God had
truly given Solomon wisdom.


# The Circle of Chalk


*A similar story is found in* The Circle of Chalk, *a classic Chinese play
of the Yuan dynasty (1259–1368), although this story involves not
prostitutes but a concubine. It was adapted six hundred years later
by the German playwright Bertolt Brecht as* The Caucasian Chalk
Circle *(1945). The following is a summary of the Chinese play.*


A penniless family was forced by their poverty to sell their
beautiful daughter, Changhi-tang, to a teahouse. There the tax
collector, Mr. Ma, bought Changhi-tang as a concubine. Within
a year, she bore him a son.

5 Mr. Ma's wife, who was childless, was so jealous of the
concubine that she poisoned her husband's tea. Then she paid
her servants to say that Changhi-tang had killed Mr. Ma and
that Mrs. Ma was the real mother of the child.

The case was brought before the new emperor, who had
10 said that he would judge all cases involving a murder. The
emperor listened carefully to the evidence. Then he drew a
circle with a piece of chalk, placed the child inside the circle,
and directed Mrs. Ma and Changhi-tang to each take hold of
one of the baby's arms. "The one who pulls the child out of the
15 circle," the emperor said, "will have him."

Mrs. Ma won, since only she would risk hurting the child.
The emperor was then certain that the concubine was the
rightful mother and that Mrs. Ma had murdered her husband.
After announcing his finding, he ordered Changhi-tang to
20 determine Mrs. Ma's punishment.

"Mrs. Ma, please prepare a cup of tea for yourself," the concubine said softly. "And let your conscience guide you in deciding what sort of tea it will be."

   a. How are the endings of the two stories different? What does Changhi-tang mean when she imposes the sentence? Do you suppose that the emperor expected her to say that?

   b. What aspects of the two stories are the same?

   c. Compare either "The Judgment of Solomon" or "The Circle of Chalk" to "Popular Mechanics." Are the stories similar or different in setting? How similar are the characters? What about the situation in the story and the way the characters react? How similar are the stories in the way the conflict is resolved?

2. What stories do you know, from the news or from your own life, about parents fighting over children? What effect did the struggle have on the children? What psychological, as well as physical, ways are there for parents to tear a child apart?

3. In class, read "Popular Mechanics" as a play. You will need a NARRATOR (12 speeches), HE (9 speeches), and SHE (12 speeches). Leave out "he said" and "she said" when these phrases occur. You may also want to have a DIRECTOR to help everyone decide where to sit or stand and when and how to speak. Several small groups can each prepare and present their version. To give more students a chance to participate, there can be a change of cast and director after "Get out of here!" (line 36).

4. Carver's story is told by a narrator who isn't a character in the story. Retell it from another point of view. How would the story be told by a nosy neighbor who has overheard the scene? By a police officer who has come to investigate in response to a call by that same neighbor? By the woman in the story when she writes to her mother about the incident? How does shifting the point of view change the story?

5. Like "No Speak English" by Cisneros, this story is told in very simple language. What other similarities can you see between the two stories? What differences are there?

6. The Public Broadcasting System (PBS) station in Seattle, Washington, has filmed an interview with Raymond Carver and Tess Gallagher. When it was shown on PBS in New York City, the program was titled "Raymond Carver: To Write and Keep Kind." The program is not presently available for purchase on video cassette; however, teachers in the U.S. may want to contact their local PBS station to see if the film is on an upcoming program schedule.

# The Unicorn in the Garden

"'The unicorn is a

mythical beast,'

she said, and

turned her back

on him."

# The Unicorn in the Garden

*James Thurber*
*(1894–1961)*

James Thurber spent his boyhood in Columbus, Ohio, in a family that was delightfully crazy. As he described the family in *My Life and Hard Times* (1933), his grandmother worried about electricity leaking out of light fixtures and wall sockets. His grandfather used to disappear for days at time, returning with late-breaking news of the Civil War, which had ended forty years before. Aunt Gracie Shoaf lived in fear of burglars. She was sure that they would come when she was asleep and use chloroform to keep her from waking up. To drive them away, she threw shoes down the hallway in the middle of the night. "Some nights," Thurber wrote, "she threw them all."

A childhood accident left Thurber blind in one eye and with only limited vision in the other. Some might say that his unusual view of the world is reflected in the style of his drawings, one of which appears with this story, as well as in the content of his stories. For over thirty years, Thurber's cartoons and stories about his family and other topics appeared in *The New Yorker,* a witty and sophisticated American magazine founded by Harold Ross. Thurber presented his version of working on *The New Yorker's* staff in *The Years with Ross* (1959). A representative selection of his work appears in *The Thurber Carnival* (1945).

Thurber stands beside Mark Twain as one of the most popular American humorists and satirists of his time. He has also joined the ancient Greek slave Aesop and the seventeenth-century French nobleman Jean de La Fontaine as a noted writer of fables. Fables, which often have animals who act like human beings as the main characters, illustrate morals that are stated directly at the end like proverbs. Thurber's *Fables for Our Time* (1940) includes "The Unicorn in the Garden." This fable illustrates a recurring theme in Thurber's work: the battle of the sexes, pitting timid but imaginative men against scheming and possessive women. In this story, a typical Thurber man finds his long-suffering existence dramatically altered. How? By the arrival of a unicorn—the medieval symbol of romantic love and sexual power.

## Uncommon Words or Meanings

**Once upon a** ("*Once upon a* sunny morning")—the conventional opening for a fairy tale is "Once upon a time." The conventional ending is "They all lived happily ever after."

**a breakfast nook** ("sat in a *breakfast nook*")—a corner of the kitchen with a small table and chairs.

**a booby** ("You are a *booby*.")—(slang) a foolish or mentally retarded person.

**a booby-hatch** ("put in the *booby hatch*")—(slang) an insane asylum, a hospital for people who are mentally ill. Thurber later makes a play on words with the verb *hatch*, to break out of a shell.

**a gloat** ("a *gloat* in her eye")—the verb *gloat* means to look at with selfish or malicious pleasure; here, the verb is used as a noun.

**a straight-jacket** ("got her into the *straight-jacket*")—a white jacket with very long sleeves used to control a mental patient.

**a jay bird** ("as crazy as a *jay bird*")—a blue jay, a common crested bird with a harsh cry. (The usual comparison is "as crazy as a loon.")

**Don't count** . . . . ("Don't count your chickens until they are hatched.")—a play on the words of the proverb the moral of the fable.

# The Unicorn in the Garden

Once upon a sunny morning a man who sat in a breakfast nook looked up from his scrambled eggs to see a white unicorn with a gold horn quietly cropping the roses in the garden. The man went up to the bedroom where his wife was still asleep and woke her. "There's a unicorn in the garden," he said. "Eating roses." She opened one unfriendly eye and looked at him. "The unicorn is a mythical beast," she said, and turned her back on him. The man walked slowly downstairs and out into the garden. The unicorn was still there; he was now browsing among the tulips. "Here, unicorn," said the man, and he pulled up a lily and gave it to him. The unicorn ate it gravely. With a high heart, because there was a unicorn in his garden, the man went upstairs and roused his wife again. "The unicorn," he said, "ate a lily." His wife sat up in bed and looked at him, coldly. "You are a booby," she said, "and I am going to have you put in the booby hatch." The man, who had never liked the words "booby" and "booby-hatch," and who liked them even less on a shining morning when there was a unicorn in the garden, thought for a moment. "We'll see about that," he said. He walked over to the door. "He has a golden horn in the middle of his forehead," he told her. Then he went back to the garden to watch the unicorn; but the unicorn had gone away. The man sat down among the roses and went to sleep.

As soon as the husband had gone out of the house, the wife got up and dressed as fast as she could. She was very excited and there was a gloat in her eye. She telephoned the police and she telephoned a psychiatrist; she told them to hurry to her house and bring a straight-jacket. When the police and the psychiatrist arrived they sat down in chairs and looked at her, with great interest. "My husband," she said, "saw a unicorn this morning." The police looked at the psychiatrist and the psychiatrist looked at the police. "He told me it ate a lily," she said. The psychiatrist looked at the police and the police looked at the psychiatrist. "He told me it had a golden horn in the middle of its forehead," she said. At a solemn signal from the psychiatrist, the police leaped from their chairs and seized the wife. They had a hard time subduing her, for she put up a terrific struggle, but they finally subdued her. Just as they got her into the straight-jacket, the husband came back into the house.

40      "Did you tell your wife you saw a unicorn?" asked the police. "Of course not," said the husband. "The unicorn is a mythical beast." "That's all I wanted to know," said the psychiatrist. "Take her away. I'm sorry, sir, but your wife is as crazy as a jay bird." So they took her away, cursing and screaming,

45 and shut her up in an institution. The husband lived happily ever after.

    *MORAL: Don't count your boobies until they are hatched.*

[1939]

1. In the first sentence, what elements of fairy tales and everyday life are juxtaposed—set side by side?

2. The unicorn eats roses and lilies. Lilies often symbolize purity; what do roses suggest? The man, we are told, has "a high heart" (line 12) because of the unicorn in his garden. What do you suppose "high heart" means? What do you think the unicorn represents?

3. Why do you think the man wakes his wife up the second time? Why do you think she reacts as she does? What does the man mean when he says (line 19), "We'll see about that"?

4. When the man goes downstairs, he finds the unicorn gone. Why do you suppose he goes to sleep rather than look for the unicorn?

5. To "have a gleam in one's eye" means to have a good idea, but the wife has "a gloat in her eye" (line 26).

   a. What does "gloat" mean, and what does the change from "gleam" to "gloat" suggest about the wife's idea and the motivation behind it?

   b. What do you think the wife has in mind when she calls the police and the psychiatrist? What do you think she expects them to do when they arrive?

   c. What is the irony—the difference between what the wife expects and what actually happens—in the result of her plan?

6. Think about the husband's actions:

   a. Surely he can hear his wife shouting. Why do you suppose he doesn't come into the house right away?

   b. What would explain his response to the psychiatrist's question?

   c. Are you surprised that he allows his wife to be "taken away cursing and screaming" (line 44)?

7. What proverb is the moral based on? What does the proverb mean? How is it appropriate to this story?

## Developing a Way with Words

Some of the words in the story—such as *garden*—are generally thought of as having pleasant associations; that is, they have a positive connotation. Other words—such as *cursing*—have unpleasant associations, a negative feeling; that is, they have a negative connotation. Divide the following words into two lists—those with positive connotations and those with negative connotations:

*booby, curse, garden, gloat, gold, heart, institution, lily, police, psychiatrist, rose (n.), scream, shining, straight jacket, struggle, subdue, sunny, unicorn.*

a. Which list can be associated with the husband? Which with the wife?

b. How do these words reflect the differences between the husband and wife? Why do you suppose these two people married?

## Making Connections

1. Is the husband crazy? Discuss the evidence for and against the view that he is.

2. How is the idea of the proverb "Don't count your chickens before they are hatched" expressed in other languages that you know?

3. What other fables do you know? In what ways is Thurber's fable similar to them? In what ways is it different?

4. Plan a dramatization of the fable. Besides a NARRATOR, how many actors will you need? This can be done as a class project, with some students preparing the script, some preparing the set, some preparing costumes and

properties, some acting, and one directing. Or, two or three small groups can each prepare and present their own simple version.

5. Arrange to see the animated film version of this story produced by the National Film Board of Canada. Then discuss and write about the differences between the way you pictured the story and the way it is presented in the film. In the United States, teachers can contact the National Film Board of Canada at 1251 Avenue of the Americas, New York, NY 10020-1173; 1-212-596-1770.)

# The Summer of the Beautiful White Horse

"If you were crazy

about horses the

way my cousin

Mourad and I

were, it wasn't

stealing."

# The Summer of the Beautiful White Horse

*William Saroyan*
*(1908–1981)*

The Armenian American writer William Saroyan grew up in poverty in Sacramento, California. After leaving school in his early teens, he worked at a variety of jobs, always with the idea of becoming a writer, and at the age of twenty-six published his first story. "The Daring Young Man on the Flying Trapeze" (1934) tells of a penniless young writer who merrily starves to death in San Francisco in the middle of the Great Depression. Like all of Saroyan's stories, that one has autobiographical elements. However, rather than starving, Saroyan became famous overnight, "the literary equivalent of a movie star," as one critic puts it. Soon he had two successful Broadway plays—*My Heart's in the Highlands* (1939) and *The Time of Your Life* (1940), both of them portraying gentle, eccentric, and homesick Armenian immigrants in California. In 1940, he also published *My Name Is Aram,* the collection of anecdotes in which "The Summer of the Beautiful White Horse" appears. Two years later, Saroyan published his best-known novel, *The Human Comedy,* also a story of Armenian immigrants in California.

Armenian history forms the background of all of these stories. This ancient kingdom of Asia Minor was located in the "fertile crescent" between the Black Sea and the Caspian Sea. Over the centuries, Armenia was invaded by one army after another and in the early 1800s, it disappeared as a country when the territory and people were divided among

Russia, Turkey, and Iran. The Turkish sultan then began a nearly successful effort to exterminate all of the Armenians under his control, by either deporting or killing them. After the great massacre of 1894, many Turkish Armenians—Saroyan's parents among them—fled Turkey and settled in California's San Joaquin Valley, raising grapes, walnuts, olives, and other crops.

In 1911, Saroyan's father died suddenly at the age of thirty-six, leaving a wife and four children, the youngest of whom was three-year-old William. Left without money, Mrs. Saroyan placed the children in an orphanage for the next five years while she worked as a maid. William's son believes that this experience left his father emotionally "frozen" in his childhood, delighting in fantasy but unable to deal with complex emotions.

"The Summer of the Beautiful White Horse" is Saroyan's reinventing of his childhood as a time of bliss rather than deep sorrow. It begins with a variation on the traditional opening of a fairy tale—"Once upon a time"—when a boy is awakened early one morning by his cousin, who is mounted on a beautiful white horse. Both boys love horses, but their families are very poor and could never buy a horse. Where has the horse come from? What will the boys do with it? And how will the matter of the horse be related to the older characters in the story, who long for their lost homelands?

## Uncommon Words or Meanings

**a streak** ("Every family has a crazy *streak* in it somewhere")—a characteristic, element.

**to be up to** ("That *is up to* the horse")—to be (someone's) responsibility to decide.

**to have a way with** ("I *have a way with* a horse")—to be skillful and persuasive in dealing with.

**to dawn on** ("suddenly *dawned on* me")—to become clear to the mind.

**hearty** ("ate a *hearty* breakfast")—abundant and nourishing.

**Assyrian** ("an *Assyrian* who, out of loneliness, had learned to speak Armenian")—a citizen of Assyria, an ancient country of Asia Minor that lost its independent existence in the eighth century B.C. In another story, Saroyan identified a well-known Armenian as "Assyrian." When asked why he had done that, Saroyan answered that "in a sense everybody in the world is an Assyrian, a remnant of a once-mighty race, now all but extinct" (*Letters from 74 rue Taitbout,* 1969).

# The Summer of the Beautiful White Horse

One day back there in the good old days when I was nine
and the world was full of every imaginable kind of magnifi-
cence, and life was still a delightful and mysterious dream, my
cousin Mourad, who was considered crazy by everybody who
5   knew him except me, came to my house at four in the morning and woke me up by tapping on the window of my room.
Aram, he said.
I jumped out of bed and looked out the window.
I couldn't believe what I saw.
10   It wasn't morning yet, but it was summer and with daybreak not many minutes around the corner of the world it was
light enough for me to know I wasn't dreaming.
My cousin Mourad was sitting on a beautiful white horse.
I stuck my head out of the window and rubbed my eyes.
15   Yes, he said in Armenian. It's a horse. You're not dreaming.
Make it quick if you want to ride.
I knew my cousin Mourad enjoyed being alive more than
anybody else who had ever fallen into the world by mistake,
but this was more than even I could believe.
20   In the first place, my earliest memories had been memories
of horses and my first longings had been longings to ride.
This was the wonderful part.
In the second place, we were poor.
This was the part that wouldn't permit me to believe what
25   I saw.
We were poor. We had no money. Our whole tribe was
poverty-stricken. Every branch of the Garoghlanian family was
living in the most amazing and comical poverty in the world.
Nobody could understand where we ever got money enough to
30   keep us with food in our bellies, not even the old men of the
family. Most important of all, though, we were famous for our
honesty. We had been famous for our honesty for something
like eleven centuries, even when we had been the wealthiest
family in what we liked to think was the world. We were proud
35   first, honest next, and after that we believed in right and
wrong. None of us would take advantage of anybody in the
world, let alone steal.

Consequently, even though I could *see* the horse, so magnificent; even though I could *smell* the horse, so lovely; even

40 though I could *hear* it breathing, so exciting; I couldn't *believe* the horse had anything to do with my cousin Mourad or with me or with any of the other members of our family, asleep or awake, because I *knew* my cousin Mourad couldn't have *bought* the horse, and if he couldn't have bought it he must

45 have *stolen* it, and I refused to believe he had stolen it.

No member of the Garoghlanian family could be a thief.

I stared first at my cousin and then at the horse. There was a pious stillness and humor in each of them which on the one hand delighted me and on the other frightened me.

50 Mourad, I said, where did you steal this horse?

Leap out of the window, he said, if you want to ride.

It was true, then. He *had* stolen the horse. There was no question about it. He had come to invite me to ride or not, as I chose.

55 Well, it seemed to me stealing a horse for a ride was not the same thing as stealing something else, such as money. For all I knew, maybe it wasn't stealing at all. If you were crazy about horses the way my cousin Mourad and I were, it wasn't stealing. It wouldn't become stealing until we offered to sell the horse,

60 which of course I knew we would never do.

Let me put on some clothes, I said.

All right, he said, but hurry.

I leaped into my clothes.

I jumped down to the yard from the window and leaped up

65 onto the horse behind my cousin Mourad.

That year we lived at the edge of town, on Walnut Avenue. Behind our house was the country: vineyards, orchards, irrigation ditches, and country roads. In less than three minutes we were on Olive Avenue, and then the horse began to trot. The air

70 was new and lovely to breathe. The feel of the horse running was wonderful. My cousin Mourad who was considered one of the craziest members of our family began to sing. I mean, he began to roar.

Every family has a crazy streak in it somewhere, and my

75 cousin Mourad was considered the natural descendant of the crazy streak in our tribe. Before him was our uncle Khosrove, an enormous man with a powerful head of black hair and the largest mustache in the San Joaquin Valley, a man so furious in

temper, so irritable, so impatient that he stopped anyone from
talking by roaring, *It is no harm; pay no attention to it.*

That was all, no matter what anybody happened to be talking about. Once it was his own son Arak running eight blocks
to the barber shop where his father was having his mustache
trimmed to tell him that their house was on fire. This man
Khosrove sat up in the chair and roared, It is no harm; pay no
attention to it. The barber said, But the boy says your house is
on fire. So Khosrove roared, Enough, it is no harm, I say.

My cousin Mourad was considered the natural descendant of this man, although Mourad's father was Zorab, who
was practical and nothing else. That's how it is in our tribe. A
man could be the father of his son's flesh, but that did not
mean that he was also the father of his spirit. The distribution
of the various kinds of spirit of our tribe had been from the
beginning capricious and vagrant.

We rode and my cousin Mourad sang. For all anybody
knew we were still in the old country where, at least according
to some of our neighbors, we belonged. We let the horse run as
long as it felt like running.

At last my cousin Mourad said, Get down. I want to ride
alone.

Will you let me ride alone? I said.

That is up to the horse, my cousin said. Get down.

The *horse* will let me ride, I said.

We shall see, he said. Don't forget that I have a way with a
horse.

Well, I said, any way you have with a horse, I have also.

For the sake of your safety, he said, let us hope so. Get
down.

All right, I said, but remember you've got to let me try to
ride alone.

I got down and my cousin Mourad kicked his heels into the
horse and shouted, *Vazire*, run. The horse stood on its hind
legs, snorted, and burst into a fury of speed that was the loveli-
est thing I had ever seen. My cousin Mourad raced the horse
across a field of dry grass to an irrigation ditch, crossed the
ditch on the horse, and five minutes later returned, dripping
wet.

The sun was coming up.

Now it's my turn to ride, I said.

120     My cousin Mourad got off the horse.

Ride, he said.

I leaped to the back of the horse and for a moment knew the awfulest fear imaginable. The horse did not move.

Kick into his muscles, my cousin Mourad said. What are
125 you waiting for? We've got to take him back before everybody in the world is up and about.

I kicked into the muscles of the horse. Once again it reared and snorted. Then it began to run. I didn't know what to do. Instead of running across the field to the irrigation ditch the
130 horse ran down the road to the vineyard of Dikran Halabian where it began to leap over vines. The horse leaped over seven vines before I fell. Then it continued running.

My cousin Mourad came running down the road.

I'm not worried about you, he shouted. We've got to get
135 that horse. You go this way and I'll go this way. If you come upon him, be kindly. I'll be near.

I continued down the road and my cousin Mourad went across the field toward the irrigation ditch.

It took him half an hour to find the horse and bring him
140 back.

All right, he said, jump on. The whole world is awake now.

What will we do? I said.

Well, he said, we'll either take him back or hide him until tomorrow morning.
145 He didn't sound worried and I knew he'd hide him and not take him back. Not for a while, at any rate.

Where will we hide him? I said.

I know a place, he said.

How long ago did you steal this horse? I said.
150     It suddenly dawned on me that he had been taking these early morning rides for some time and had come for me this morning only because he knew how much I longed to ride.

Who said anything about stealing a horse? he said.

Anyhow, I said, how long ago did you begin riding every
155 morning?

Not until this morning, he said.

Are you telling the truth? I said.

Of course not, he said, but if we are found out, that's what you're to say. I don't want both of us to be liars. All you know
160 is that we started riding this morning.

All right, I said.

He walked the horse quietly to the barn of a deserted vineyard which at one time had been the pride of a farmer named Fetvajian. There were some oats and dry alfalfa in the barn.

We began walking home.

165 It wasn't easy, he said, to get the horse to behave so nicely. At first it wanted to run wild, but, as I've told you, I have a way with a horse. I can get it to want to do anything *I* want it to do. Horses understand me.

How do you do it? I said.

170 I have an understanding with a horse, he said.

Yes, but what sort of an understanding? I said.

A simple and honest one, he said.

Well, I said, I wish I knew how to reach an understanding like that with a horse.

175 You're still a small boy, he said. When you get to be thirteen you'll know how to do it.

I went home and ate a hearty breakfast.

That afternoon my uncle Khosrove came to our house for coffee and cigarettes. He sat in the parlor, sipping and smoking 180 and remembering the old country. Then another visitor arrived, a farmer named John Byro, an Assyrian who, out of loneliness, had learned to speak Armenian. My mother brought the lonely visitor coffee and tobacco and he rolled a cigarette and sipped and smoked, and then at last, sighing sadly, he said, My white 185 horse which was stolen last month is still gone. I cannot understand it.

My uncle Khosrove became very irritated and shouted, It's no harm. What is the loss of a horse? Haven't we all lost a homeland? What is this crying over a horse?

190 That may be all right for you, a city dweller, to say, John Byro said, but what of my surrey? What good is a surrey without a horse?

Pay no attention to it, my uncle Khosrove roared.

I walked ten miles to get here, John Byro said.

195 You have legs, my uncle Khosrove shouted.

My left leg pains me, the farmer said.

Pay no attention to it, my uncle Khosrove roared.

That horse cost me sixty dollars, the farmer said.

I spit on money, my uncle Khosrove said.

200 He got up and stalked out of the house, slamming the screen door.

My mother explained.

He has a gentle heart, she said. It is simply that he is home-sick and such a large man.

205     The farmer went away and I ran over to my cousin Mourad's house.

He was sitting under a peach tree, trying to repair the hurt wing of a young robin which could not fly. He was talking to the bird.

210     What is it? he said.

The farmer, John Byro, I said. He visited our house. He wants his horse. You've had it a month. I want you to promise not to take it back until I learn to ride.

It will take you *a year* to learn to ride, my cousin Mourad
215 said.

We could keep the horse a year, I said.

My cousin Mourad leaped to his feet.

What? he roared. Are you inviting a member of the Garogh-lanian family to steal? The horse must go back to its true
220 owner.

When? I said.

In six months at the latest, he said.

He threw the bird into the air. The bird tried hard, almost fell twice, but at last flew away, high and straight.

225     Early every morning for two weeks my cousin Mourad and I took the horse out of the barn of the deserted vineyard where we were hiding it and rode it, and every morning the horse, when it was my turn to ride alone, leaped over grape vines and small trees and threw me and ran away. Nevertheless, I hoped
230 in time to learn to ride the way my cousin Mourad rode.

One morning on the way to Fetvajian's deserted vineyard we ran into the farmer John Byro who was on his way to town.

Let me do the talking, my cousin Mourad said. I have a way with farmers.

235     Good morning, John Byro, my cousin Mourad said to the farmer.

The farmer studied the horse eagerly.

Good morning, sons of my friends, he said. What is the name of your horse?

240     *My Heart*, my cousin Mourad said in Armenian.

A lovely name, John Byro said, for a lovely horse. I could swear it is the horse that was stolen from me many weeks ago. May I look into its mouth?

Of course, Mourad said.

245 The farmer looked into the mouth of the horse.

Tooth for tooth, he said. I would swear it *is* my horse if I didn't know your parents. The fame of your family for honesty is well known to me. Yet the horse is the twin of my horse. A suspicious man would believe his eyes instead of his heart.

250 Good day, my young friends.

Good day, John Byro, my cousin Mourad said.

Early the following morning we took the horse to John Byro's vineyard and put it in the barn. The dogs followed us around without making a sound.

255 The dogs, I whispered to my cousin Mourad. I thought they would bark.

They would at somebody else, he said. I have a way with dogs.

My cousin Mourad put his arms around the horse, pressed
260 his nose into the horse's nose, patted it, and then we went away.

That afternoon John Byro came to our house in his surrey and showed my mother the horse that had been stolen and returned.

265 I do not know what to think, he said. The horse is stronger than ever. Better-tempered, too. I thank God.

My uncle Khosrove, who was in the parlor, became irritated and shouted, Quiet, man, quiet. Your horse has been returned. Pay no attention to it.

[1940]

## Understanding the Story

1. Why is Aram so surprised when his cousin invites him to go horseback riding? What are some examples of his excitement? How does he justify their having the horse (lines 55–60)?

2. Identify the speaker and situation for each of the following statements. How does each statement reflect the personality of the speaker? Can you find one or two more statements that are typical of each of the characters?

a. "Don't forget that I have a way with a horse." (lines 104–5)

b. For all anybody knew we were still in the old country where, at least according to some of our neighbors, we belonged. (lines 95–97)

c. "What is the loss of a horse? Haven't we all lost a homeland?" (lines 188–89)

d. "I walked ten miles to get here." (line 194)

3. Aram, Mourad, and John Byro each have a different relationship with the horse.

   a. What does the horse mean to each of them? Why? For example, why do you think Cousin Mourad names the horse "My Heart"?

   b. How does the horse react to each of them? Why?

4. Woven into the story of the boys and the horse, the narrator describes two other incidents.

   a. What does the incident in the barber shop (lines 82–87) show about uncle Khosrove? How is that information related to the story of the horse?

   b. What does the incident of the robin with a broken wing (lines 207–24) show about cousin Mourad? How is that information related to the story of the horse?

5. What do John Byro and uncle Khosrove have in common? How are they different from each other? Why is uncle Khosrove so unsympathetic to the farmer?

6. When John Byro meets the boys, what do you think he means by saying (lines 248–49), "A suspicious man would believe his eyes instead of his heart"?

7. What provides the happy ending for this story? From his final comment, do you think uncle Khosrove believes in happy endings?

## Developing a Way with Words

1. In the following sentences, how does Saroyan use irony (an unexpected contrast), hyperbole (deliberate exaggeration), and flawed logic to create humor?

   a. Every branch of the Garoghlanian family was living in the most amazing and comical poverty in the world. (lines 27–28)

   b. We had been famous for our honesty for something like eleven centuries, even when we had been the wealthiest family in what we liked to think was the world. (lines 32–34)

   c. Well, it seemed to me that stealing a horse to ride was not the same thing as stealing something else, such as money. For all I knew, maybe it wasn't stealing at all. If you were crazy about horses the way my cousin Mourad and I were, it wasn't stealing. It wouldn't be stealing until we offered to sell the horse, which of course I knew we would never do. (lines 55–60)

2. Throughout the story, there are references to "the world," for example "daybreak not many minutes around the corner of the world" (lines 10–11) and "The whole world is awake now" (line 141), as well as the sentence in 1b above. Go through the story to find other examples. What does Aram mean by "the world"?

3. Look at the opening paragraph. It's a single sentence of sixty-eight words. That's a normal length for a paragraph but most unusual for a single sentence. Divide the paragraph into several sentences. Does that make the paragraph easier to read? What other difference does it make? Why do you think the author made that sentence so long?

## M aking Connections

1. Do you think the characters in the story are meant to be realistic? Why or why not?

2. Do you agree with their families that the behavior of Mourad and uncle Khosrove is "crazy"? In what way or ways are they different from the people around them? How are they different from each other? How are they alike?

3. Aram says (lines 90–92), "A man could be the father of his son's flesh, but that did not mean that he was also the father of his spirit." What do you think he means by that? Could people in your family be used to illustrate the same idea?

4. The older men in the story are homesick for their native countries, while the boys, who speak Armenian but are growing up in the United States, are enjoying all of the possibilities of their new homeland. How typical is that of immigrant groups?

5. When you were a child, did you ever have a crazy adventure? If so, what was it? What was the outcome?

6. This story is like "The Unicorn in the Garden" in that it has an unusually long opening sentence and is humorous in tone. How else are the stories alike? In what ways are they different?

# Samuel

"The boys opened their eyes wide at each other and laughed."

# Samuel

*Grace Paley*
*(born 1922)*

Grace Paley was born in the Bronx, one of the five boroughs of New York City. Like many other Bronx residents at the time, her parents were Russian Jewish immigrants. The family members were lively story-tellers in three languages—Russian, Yiddish, and English. "I loved to listen," Paley has said of her childhood, "and soon I loved to talk and tell." She entered Hunter College at the age of fifteen and later attended New York University but never completed a degree. "I really went to school on poetry," Paley later explained. "I learned whatever I know about language and craft from writing poems."

Paley moved from writing poetry to writing stories during her years as a wife, mother, and political activist in the part of Manhattan (another borough of New York) called Greenwich Village. In the mid-twentieth century, "the Village" was favored by artists and political liberals. The streets were narrow, the buildings were not more than five stories high, and people talked comfortably with their neighbors. Meeting other women in the shops, on the playgrounds, and at anti-war demonstrations, Paley realized that they were not represented in contemporary literature. She began to write stories to give these women "a voice," winning high praise for her first collection, *The Little Disturbances of Man* (1959). Then Paley put aside literary concerns and devoted her energies to supporting the peace movement and campaigning for the nuclear freeze, environmentalism, feminism, and prison reform. (Paley has described herself as a "somewhat combative pacifist and cooperative anarchist.")

Despite her total of only three books in thirty years—the second and third are *Enormous Changes at the Last Minute* (1974), which includes "Samuel," and *Later the Same Day* (1985), Paley has become a writer with a large reputation. (The three were reissued in a single volume in 1994.) Since the early 1960s, Paley has taught university courses in writing because, as she explains, "teaching always puts you in contact with new historical experience—not just with people but with the nature of their lives." Paley has a gift for understanding this nature and capturing it in fiction. Beneath the "tough-kid" New York voice of the stories is an unfailing interest in and understanding of the enormous variety of people who comprise New York City. And through this understanding, Paley identifies feelings and experiences that every reader can share.

For "Samuel," Paley has chosen a location where the widest variety of people meet—the subway. The subway train in this story is traveling from Manhattan (the island that many people—including the men in the story—mean when they refer to "New York") to the Bronx, the northernmost of the city's five boroughs. To follow the story, it's useful to know something about the tracks and trains of the subway system. First, the tracks are underground in almost all of Manhattan but are elevated in the Bronx. Second, the cars of the subway train are joined by couplings similar to freight trains or passenger trains. A foot or so above these couplings are steel platforms that allow passengers to walk from one car to the next. (The doors at the ends of the cars began to be locked as air-conditioning was introduced in preparation for the 1964 World's Fair.) On either side of these platforms, at waist-height, are chains to keep passengers from falling between the cars. Come for a subway ride to meet Samuel and his friends, with the warning that Paley has the power to make her readers both laugh and cry in the course of one story.

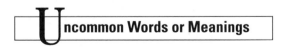

## Uncommon Words or Meanings

**to take a bow** ("the ones who climb a wall and *take a bow* at the top")—(idiom) to acknowledge applause or verbal admiration by bowing.

**a super** ("where even the *super* hates to go")—New York City abbreviation for "superintendent," a building caretaker.

**to jiggle** ("*jiggle* and hop on the platform between the locked doors of the subway cars")—(informal) to move sideways and up and down (as the subway train moves rapidly along the tracks).

**from New York to Rockaway Beach** ("had ridden the tail of a speeding truck *from New York to Rockaway Beach*")—a distance of twelve or thirteen miles. Here "New York" means Manhattan; Rockaway Beach is in the borough of Queens, also part of New York City.

**Eighth Avenue and Fifteenth Street . . . Twenty-third [Street] and the [Hudson] river** ("Starting at *Eighth Avenue and Fifteenth Street,* he would get to some specified place, maybe *Twenty-third and the river*")—a distance of slightly over a mile. This is a commercial part of Manhattan with many warehouses and a lot of truck traffic.

**logging** ("a film at school called *The Romance of* Logging")—cutting down trees for lumber. At the time of the film, North American loggers, or lumberjacks, had one of the world's most dangerous jobs: as logs floated downriver to a sawmill, the lumberjacks could be called on to walk from one free-floating log to another to locate and loosen the key log in a logjam.

**way high over the Bronx** ("we're out of the tunnel and *way high over the Bronx*")—The train is going north from Manhattan, under the Harlem River, to the Bronx, where it runs as an elevated train.

**fresh** ("was afraid they'd be *fresh* and laugh at her")—impolite, especially used of children.

**rat-tat-tatted** ("then they *rat-tat-tatted* the shatterproof glass pane like machine guns")—made a sound like a machine gun.

**shatterproof** ("rat-tat-tatted the *shatterproof* glass pane)—treated to resist **shattering,** breaking violently into small pieces.

**a motorman** ("For some reason known only to the *motorman,* the train began a sudden slowdown.")—the "driver" in the first car of a subway train.

**to pound** ("Samuel laughed the hardest and *pounded* Alfred's back")—to hit heavily and repeatedly.

**the emergency cord** ("where he pulled *the emergency cord*")—the rope at the end of the subway car that enabled a passenger to stop the train.

# Samuel

Some boys are very tough. They're afraid of nothing. They are the ones who climb a wall and take a bow at the top. Not only are they brave on the roof, but they make a lot of noise in the darkest part of the cellar where even the super hates to go.
5 They also jiggle and hop on the platform between the locked doors of the subway cars.

Four boys are jiggling on the swaying platform. Their names are Alfred, Calvin, Samuel, and Tom. The men and the women in the cars on either side watch them. They don't like
10 them to jiggle or jump but don't want to interfere. Of course some of the men in the cars were once brave boys like these. One of them had ridden the tail of a speeding truck from New York to Rockaway Beach without getting off, without his sore fingers losing hold. Nothing happened to him then or later. He
15 had made a compact with other boys who preferred to watch: Starting at Eighth Avenue and Fifteenth Street, he would get to some specified place, maybe Twenty-third and the river, by hopping the tops of moving trucks. This was hard to do when one truck turned a corner in the wrong direction and the near-
20 est truck was a couple of feet too high. He made three or four starts before succeeding. He had gotten this idea from a film at school called *The Romance of Logging*. He had finished high school, married a good friend, was in a responsible job and going to night school.

25 These two men and others looked at the four boys jumping and jiggling on the platform and thought, It must be fun to ride that way, especially now the weather is nice and we're out of the tunnel and way high over the Bronx. Then they thought, These kids do seem to be acting sort of stupid. They *are* little.
30 Then they thought of some of the brave things they had done when they were boys and jiggling didn't seem so risky.

The ladies in the car became very angry when they looked at the four boys. Most of them brought their brows together and hoped the boys could see their extreme disapproval. One of the
35 ladies wanted to get up and say, Be careful you dumb kids, get off that platform or I'll call a cop. But three of the boys were Negroes and the fourth was something else she couldn't tell for

sure. She was afraid they'd be fresh and laugh at her and embarrass her. She wasn't afraid they'd hit her, but she was afraid of
40  embarrassment. Another lady thought, Their mothers never know where they are. It wasn't true in this particular case. Their mothers all knew that they had gone to see the missile exhibit on Fourteenth Street.

Out on the platform, whenever the train accelerated, the
45  boys would raise their hands and point them up to the sky to act like rockets going off, then they rat-tat-tatted the shatterproof glass pane like machine guns, although no machine guns had been exhibited.

For some reason known only to the motorman, the train
50  began a sudden slowdown. The lady who was afraid of embarrassment saw the boys jerk forward and backward and grab the swinging guard chains. She had her own boy at home. She stood up with determination and went to the door. She slid it open and said, "You boys will be hurt. You'll be killed. I'm
55  going to call the conductor if you don't just go into the next car and sit down and be quiet."

Two of the boys said, "Yes'm," and acted as though they were about to go. Two of them blinked their eyes a couple of times and pressed their lips together. The train resumed its
60  speed. The door slid shut, parting the lady and the boys. She leaned against the side door because she had to get off at the next stop.

The boys opened their eyes wide at each other and laughed. The lady blushed. The boys looked at her and laughed
65  harder. They began to pound each other's back. Samuel laughed the hardest and pounded Alfred's back until Alfred coughed and the tears came. Alfred held tight to the chain hook. Samuel pounded him even harder when he saw the tears. He said, "Why you bawling? You a baby, huh?" and
70  laughed. One of the men whose boyhood had been much more watchful than brave became angry. He stood up straight and looked at the boys for a couple of seconds. Then he walked in a citizenly way to the end of the car, where he pulled the emergency cord. Almost at once, with a terrible hiss, the pressure
75  of air abandoned the brakes and the wheels were caught and held.

People standing in the most secure places fell forward, then backward. Samuel had let go of his hold on the chain so he could pound Tom as well as Alfred. All the passengers in the

80　car whipped back and forth, but he pitched only forward and fell head first to be crushed and killed between the cars.

The train had stopped hard, halfway into the station, and the conductor called at once for the trainmen who knew about this kind of death and how to take the body from the wheels
85　and brakes. There was silence except for passengers from other cars who asked, What happened! What happened! The ladies waited around wondering if he might be an only child. The men recalled other afternoons with very bad endings. The little boys stayed close to each other, leaning and touching
90　shoulders and arms and legs.

When the policeman knocked at the door and told her about it, Samuel's mother began to scream. She screamed all day and moaned all night, though the doctors tried to quiet her with pills.
95　Oh, oh, she hopelessly cried. She did not know how she could ever find another boy like that one. However, she was a young woman and she became pregnant. Then for a few months she was hopeful. The child born to her was a boy. They brought him to be seen and nursed. She smiled. But immedi-
100　ately she saw that this baby wasn't Samuel. She and her husband together have had other children, but never again will a boy exactly like Samuel be known.

[1960]

## Understanding the Story

1. "Some boys are very tough. They're afraid of nothing" (line 1). In the first two paragraphs, what are the ways that a city boy can show he is "tough"? Which of these ways are harmless? Which are dangerous? Why?

2. Both the men and the women watching Samuel and his friends knew that riding between subway cars is dangerous; however, all of the adults hesitated to interfere. Why?

   a. How did the memories of their own childhoods keep the men from saying anything?

   b. How were the women's reasons for not interfering different from the men's?

3. At several points in the story, there is an unexpected difference—an ironic contrast—between someone's intention and the result. In the following examples, how does a well-intentioned action lead to a dangerous result?

   a. When he was a schoolboy, one of the men in the subway car had seen an educational film about the logging industry. What activity did the film inspire?

   b. Samuel and his friends visited a missile exhibit. What action did they imitate in the subway car on the way home?

   c. One of the women in an adjacent subway car scolded the boys to make them stop acting dangerously. How did the boys respond?

4. Two of the women had preconceived ideas about the boys. How accurate were the women's ideas that the boys would "be fresh and laugh and embarrass her" (lines 38–39) and that "Their mothers never know where they are" (lines 40–41)? What was the basis for the women's ideas?

5. Early in the story (lines 14–15), a distinction is made between boys who are really brave and those who aren't: "He [the boy who jumped from one moving truck to another] had made a compact with other boys who preferred to watch."

   a. Which kind of boy was Samuel?

   b. As a youngster, which kind of boy was the man who finally pulled the emergency cord?

   c. What emotion led the man to pull the cord? What result did he anticipate?

6. How did Samuel die? Would the reader be more or less horrified if Paley had described the sight or sound of the accident in detail? Why?

7. How did each of the following people or groups of people react to Samuel's death? What might account for the difference in their reactions?

a. The conductor and the trainmen.

b. The "passengers from other cars" who hadn't seen the accident.

c. "The ladies" in the two cars who had seen the accident.

d. "The men" in the two cars who had seen the accident.

e. Samuel's friends, who, after the accident, are for the first time described as "little boys." (line 89)

8. How did Samuel's mother react to the news? Why do you suppose we're not told of his father's reaction?

9. How would the story be different if the last two sentences had been left out?

 **D**eveloping a Way with Words

In each of the following sentences, find the word or group of words that refers to time. You will notice that Paley has shifted these adverbs and adverbial phrases from their usual place. (Adverbial phrases commonly come at the end of a sentence, and single adverbs ending in *-ly* often come between the subject and verb.) When the sentences are rewritten to make them more ordinary (the examples in parentheses), how does the emphasis change?

1. Then for a few months she was hopeful. (*Rewritten:* Then she was hopeful for a few months.)

2. But immediately she saw that this baby wasn't Samuel. (*Rewritten:* But she immediately saw that this baby wasn't Samuel.)

3. She and her husband together have had other children, but never again will a boy exactly like Samuel be known. (*Rewritten:* She and her husband have had other children together, but there will never be another boy just like Samuel.)

# M aking Connections

1. Paley devotes a great deal of the story to the differences in temperament between boys, emphasizing the way some boys exhibit their bravery.

   a. Does she want her readers to admire boys who take chances or, like "the ladies," to disapprove of them? What helps a reader to sense how she feels?

   b. How do you feel about boys who, like Samuel, like to take chances? Why?

2. In an urban setting that you know, how do boys nowadays show that they are tough and brave? When you were a child, how did boys show that they were tough and brave? What did girls need to prove? What dangerous games do you remember playing as a child?

3. In pairs or small groups, make a list of people who could be considered responsible for Samuel's death. Give the reason for each person (or group of people). Then order the list with "most responsible" at the top. Finally, as a class, compare all the lists, discussing the reasons for the choice of people on the list and the order in which they are placed.

4. Which people, or groups of people, do you think were most affected by Samuel's death? How do you think his death affected them? Why?

5. In class, act out the story. You will need several NARRATORS, perhaps one narrator for every two of the eleven paragraphs in the story, with the last narrator reading three paragraphs.
   The other parts are FIRST LADY (read both her thoughts, lines 35–36, and her words, lines 54–56) and SECOND LADY (read her thought, lines 40–41). ALFRED, CALVIN, SAMUEL, and TOM all gesture, make noises

like machine guns, and laugh; ALFRED also coughs (lines 66–67) and SAMUEL speaks (line 69). The FIRST MAN reads lines 12–24, beginning with "One of them . . . ." The SECOND MAN reads the thought beginning "These kids . . . " (line 29). Others in the class can be PASSENGERS, the MOTORMAN, the POLICEMAN, and SAMUEL'S MOTHER. The teacher can serve as the DIRECTOR, helping everyone decide where to sit or stand and when and how to speak.

6. How is the adventure in this story similar to and different from that in "The Summer of the Beautiful White Horse" by Saroyan?

7. Paley has said that everyone in her family was a good storyteller. Who are the best storytellers in your family or among other people you know? Are you a good story-teller yourself? What qualities make a good storyteller?

# The Chaser

"Young people

who need a love

potion very

seldom have five

thousand dollars."

# The Chaser

## John Collier
## (1901–1980)

The short stories of John Collier, who was born and educated in England, were regularly published in leading American magazines from the 1930s through the 1950s. During that time, Collier also worked as a screenwriter in Hollywood. (He wrote the first draft for the script of *The African Queen,* which starred Humphrey Bogart and Katharine Hepburn.) Collier's stories have been collected in several books (including *Fancies and Goodnights,* 1951, and *The Best of John Collier,* 1975) and they continue to appear in short-story anthologies in English and in translation. A comprehensive study of his life and work appears in *John Collier* by Betty Richardson (1981).

As novelist Anthony Burgess notes in his introduction to *The Best of John Collier,* both the film scripts and short stories show Collier's skill in writing dialogue and his gift for sharp observation. Burgess also remarks that Collier "makes literature out of the intrusion of fantasy, or quiet horror, into a real world closely observed," often making fun of both the Hollywood films and the popular fiction of his day, particularly their portrayal of romantic love.

In "The Chaser," a young man adores a woman who doesn't return his affection. Though he is "as nervous as a kitten," the young man goes in search of a way to win the young woman's love. (Like many of Collier's light-hearted heroines, she is named Diana, after the Roman goddess of the hunt. Diana was also the goddess of the moon, which was believed to affect emotions.) What do you suppose the fantasy element in this story will be? A "chaser" is a mild beverage drunk after a stronger one, such as beer used to "chase" whiskey. What do you think the first drink will be in this story? And the chaser?

This is a story filled with irony—an intended or unintended contrast between what is expected and what actually happens, or between what is said and what is meant. For example, the young man wants to change the young woman without considering all the possible effects of the changes. As you read, look for other examples.

## Uncommon Words or Meanings

**Pell Street** ("in the neighbourhood of *Pell Street*")—a principal street in New York's Chinatown.

**gay** ("no matter how *gay* and giddy she is")—light-hearted, cheerful.

**giddy** ("gay and *giddy*")—frivolously happy.

**a draught** ("to sit in a *draught*")—a current of air (*draft* in American spelling).

**a siren** ("some *siren* has caught you")—a seductive woman; a reference to the minor goddesses of Greek mythology who lived on an island and used their enchanting voices to lure sailors to their deaths upon the rocks.

**grounds** ("give you the least . . . *grounds* for—uneasiness")—(usually plural) basis or reason for a thought or action; commonly used in the phrase "grounds for divorce."

***Au revoir***—(French) "Good-bye until we meet again."

Alan Austen, as nervous as a kitten, went up certain dark and creaky stairs in the neighbourhood of Pell Street, and peered about for a long time on the dim landing before he found the name he wanted written obscurely on one of the doors.

He pushed open this door, as he had been told to do, and found himself in a tiny room, which contained no furniture but a plain kitchen table, a rocking-chair, and an ordinary chair. On one of the dirty buff-coloured walls were a couple of shelves, containing in all perhaps a dozen bottles and jars.

An old man sat in the rocking-chair, reading a newspaper. Alan, without a word, handed him the card he had been given. "Sit down, Mr. Austen," said the old man very politely. "I am glad to make your acquaintance."

"Is it true," asked Alan, "that you have a certain mixture that has—er—quite extraordinary effects?"

"My dear sir," replied the old man, "my stock in trade is not very large—I don't deal in laxatives and teething mixtures—but such as it is, it is varied. I think nothing I sell has effects which could be precisely described as ordinary."

"Well, the fact is—" began Alan.

"Here, for example," interrupted the old man, reaching for a bottle from the shelf. "Here is a liquid as colourless as water, almost tasteless, quite imperceptible in coffee, milk, wine, or any other beverage. It is also quite imperceptible to any known method of autopsy."

"Do you mean it is a poison?" cried Alan, very much horrified.

"Call it a glove-cleaner if you like," said the old man indifferently. "Maybe it will clean gloves. I have never tried. One might call it a life-cleaner. Lives need cleaning sometimes."

"I want nothing of that sort," said Alan.

"Probably it is just as well," said the old man. "Do you know the price of this? For one teaspoonful, which is sufficient, I ask five thousand dollars. Never less. Not a penny less."

"I hope all your mixtures are not as expensive," said Alan apprehensively.

"Oh dear, no," said the old man. "It would be no good charging that sort of price for a love potion, for example. Young people who need a love potion very seldom have five thousand dollars. Otherwise they would not need a love potion."

"I am glad to hear that," said Alan.

"I look at it like this," said the old man. "Please a customer with one article, and he will come back when he needs another. Even if it *is* more costly. He will save up for it, if necessary."

"So," said Alan, "you really do sell love potions?"

"If I did not sell love potions," said the old man, reaching for another bottle, "I should not have mentioned the other matter to you. It is only when one is in a position to oblige that one can afford to be so confidential."

"And these potions," said Alan. "They are not just—just—er—"

"Oh, no," said the old man. "Their effects are permanent, and extend far beyond the mere casual impulse. But they include it. Oh, yes, they include it. Bountifully, insistently. Everlastingly."

"Dear me!" said Alan, attempting a look of scientific detachment. "How very interesting!"

"But consider the spiritual side," said the old man.

"I do indeed," said Alan.

"For indifference," said the old man, "they substitute devotion. For scorn, adoration. Give one tiny measure of this to the young lady—its flavour is imperceptible in orange juice, soup, or cocktails—and however gay and giddy she is, she will change altogether. She will want nothing but solitude and you."

"I can hardly believe it," said Alan. "She is so fond of parties."

"She will not like them anymore," said the old man. "She will be afraid of the pretty girls you may meet."

"She will actually be jealous?" cried Alan in a rapture. "Of me?"

"Yes, she will want to be everything to you."

"She is already. Only she doesn't care about it."

"She will, when she has taken this. She will care intensely. You will be her sole interest in life."

"Wonderful!" cried Alan.

"She will want to know all you do," said the old man. "All

that has happened to you during the day. Every word of it. She
will want to know what you are thinking about, why you smile
suddenly, why you are looking sad."

"That is love!" cried Alan.

"Yes," said the old man. "How carefully she will look after
you! She will never allow you to be tired, to sit in a draught, to
neglect your food. If you are an hour late, she will be terrified.
She will think you are killed, or that some siren has caught
you."

"I can hardly imagine Diana like that!" cried Alan, over-
whelmed with joy.

"You will not have to use your imagination," said the old
man. "And, by the way, since there are always sirens, if by any
chance you *should*, later on, slip a little, you need not worry.
She will forgive you, in the end. She will be terribly hurt, of
course, but she will forgive you—in the end."

"That will not happen," said Alan fervently.

"Of course not," said the old man. "But if it did, you need
not worry. She would never divorce you. Oh, no! And, of
course, she herself will never give you the least, the very least
grounds for—uneasiness."

"And how much," said Alan, "is this wonderful mixture?"

"It is not as dear," said the old man, "as the glove-cleaner,
or life-cleaner, as I sometimes call it. No. That is five thousand
dollars, never a penny less. One has to be older than you are,
to indulge in that sort of thing. One has to save up for it."

"But the love potion?" said Alan.

"Oh, that," said the old man, opening the drawer in the
kitchen table, and taking out a tiny, rather dirty-looking phial.
"That is just a dollar."

"I can't tell you how grateful I am," said Alan, watching him
fill it.

"I like to oblige," said the old man. "Then customers come
back, later in life, when they are rather better off, and want
more expensive things. Here you are. You will find it very
effective."

"Thank you again," said Alan. "Good-bye."

"*Au revoir*," said the old man.

[1940]

1. Referring to Pell Street, a real place, makes the setting seem real. What details make the setting seem mysterious? When Alan is described as being "as nervous as a kitten" (line 1), what picture of him does that create?

2. Why has Alan gone to see the old man? How does the old man know Alan's name? Since, as the old man says, he sells only a few products, why doesn't he respond directly to Alan's first question? Doesn't he understand what Alan wants?

3. What are the four qualities of the first product that the old man describes? What other quality is implied? Why is the product so expensive? Why do you think the old man keeps coming back to it even though Alan says he is not interested?

4. The old man refers to "the young lady" (lines 63–64).

   a. No woman has been mentioned previously; what "young lady" does he mean?

   b. What do Alan's comments tell the old man, and the reader, about Diana?

   c. What is the implication of her name? (Do you think the name "Jane" or "Mary" would have the same effect on the reader?)

   d. Why is Alan so attracted to Diana? Why do you suppose she isn't equally attracted to him?

5. Describe the physical and "spiritual" effects of the love potion. How will they change Diana's life? How will they change Alan's life? What is the difference between the outcome Alan expects and that predicted by the old man?

6. How is it ironic (providing an unintended contradiction) that Alan is in love with Diana as she is now but wants to change her?

7. Discuss the meaning—direct and indirect—of each of the following statements. Which of them could be described as having an unexpected twist, as being ironic?

a. "Lives need cleaning sometimes." (line 31)

b. "Young people who need a love potion very seldom have five thousand dollars. Otherwise they would not need a love potion." (lines 40–42)

c. "And, by the way, since there are always sirens, if by any chance you *should*, later on, slip a little, you need not worry." (lines 91–92)

d. "She will forgive you, in the end. She will be terribly hurt, of course, but she will forgive you—in the end." (lines 93–94)

e. "*Au revoir.*" (line 116)

## Developing a Way with Words

Anthony Burgess has praised Collier for having "all the script-writer's virtues—intense economy, characterization through speech, the sharp camera-eye of observation."

1. Test this story for "intense economy" by asking two questions: Could any of the descriptive passages be left out? Could any of the speeches be shortened? If so, which?

2. Test for "characterization through speech" by asking this: How are the personalities of Alan and the old man revealed by the way they talk? Give examples.

3. Test for "sharp camera eye of observation" by asking this: Where is the description of setting or behavior so clear that the reader can see every important detail? Give examples.

## Making Connections

1. What is Alan's idea of true love? Do you think the old man shares the same idea? Why or why not? In your

opinion, is the kind of love Alan believes in a good basis for marriage? Why or why not?

2. How have American movies have changed since the time Collier was writing? Do they still present the view of romantic love that Alan believes in? In the films you have seen and books you have read, what is the most common picture of a love relationship?

3. If Alan could talk to the husband from "The Unicorn in the Garden," what do you think the two men might say to each other?

4. Have you ever loved someone who didn't love you? If so, given the opportunity, would you have given that person a love potion like the one Alan bought? Why or why not?

5. In class, read the story as a play. There are three characters: the NARRATOR (reading the first two paragraphs), the OLD MAN (22 speeches, leaving out the various forms of "he said"), and ALAN (21 speeches, again leaving out "he said"). This can be done effectively in small groups, with "cast changes" after every ten speeches.

6. Discuss the comments of Anthony Burgess quoted in the introduction in relation to this story. What elements of "The Chaser" are realistic? What elements are fantastic? Are there elements of "quiet horror"? If so, what are they?

7. What do you think will become of Alan and Diana? Write a brief scene that takes place after the close of this story—for example, when Alan gives Diana the love potion, the first time he suggests going to a party, or a night when he comes home late after an adventure with a siren.

# The Brown House

". . . and everyone knows that a white-snake dream is a sure omen of good luck in games of chance."

# The Brown House

*Hisaye Yamamoto*
*(born 1921)*

Hisaye Yamamoto, one of the pioneers of Asian American literature, was born in Redondo Beach, California shortly after World War I. At the beginning of the U.S. involvement in World War II, which came with the Japanese attack on Pearl Harbor in December 1941, both Issei (first-generation Japanese immigrants like Yamamoto's parents) and Nisei (their American-born children) were suspected of being sympathetic to Japan. Even though they were American citizens, these people were forced to give up their homes and businesses—most of which were in some way related to raising fruits and vegetables—and to spend the war in camps called "relocation centers" in remote areas away from the coast. The effect on many was devastating, for they felt betrayed by the country they had come to love. (Yamamoto's brother was one of the young Japanese American men who volunteered for the U.S. Army. Sent to fight in Europe, the Nisei unit was among the most decorated in the history of the U.S. armed forces. Yamamoto's brother was killed in action.)

In the Arizona camp where her family was interned, Yamamoto wrote for the camp newspaper and published a serialized murder mystery. After the war, she became a "rewrite man" and columnist for the *Los Angeles Tribune,* a black weekly. Her first acceptance by a literary magazine came in 1948; two years later a John Hay Whitney Foundation Fellowship provided her an opportunity to write full-time for a year. Soon she had three award-winning stories: "Seventeen Syllables" (1949), "Yoneko's Earthquake" (l951), and "The Brown House" (1951). Several years later, while volunteering at a Catholic Worker rehabilitation farm on Staten Island, a part of New York City, Yamamoto met and married Anthony DeSoto. Together with her adopted son, they returned to Los Angeles, where four more sons were born to them. Yamamoto continued to write stories that were widely anthologized. "I guess I write (aside from compulsion), to reaffirm certain basic truths which seem to get lost in the shuffle from generation to generation," she has said. "If the reader is entertained, wonderful. If he learns something, that's a bonus."* Forty years after the first appearance of Yamamoto's work in a literary magazine, *Seventeen Syllables and Other Stories* was published by Women of Color Press.

"The Brown House" illustrates several themes that are characteristic of Yamamoto's work. As these themes are identified by King-Kok Cheung in her introduction to *Seventeen Syllables,* the first is "the interaction among various ethnic groups in the American West." What ethnic groups, besides Japanese Americans, do you suppose there will be in the story? The second theme is "the precarious relationship between Issei parents and their Nisei children." How delicate and difficult are the relations between the first and second generations of any immigrant group? The final theme is the hopes of first-generation Japanese immigrants in contrast to the difficulties and frustrations that they face in America. In "The Brown House," Mr. Hattori finds an escape from the difficulties and frustrations of his life in gambling. What do you suppose his problems are? Mrs. Hattori is very likely one of the "picture brides" sent from Japan to marry the Japanese bachelors who had established themselves in the U.S. What hopes do you suppose she had at the beginning of her marriage? What frustrations do you suppose she faces? And what could be the significance of the brown house?

*Quoted in Kai-yu Hsu and Helen Palubinskas, eds., *Asian American Authors* (1972).

## Uncommon Words or Meanings

**a clapboard** ("a large but simple *clapboard*")—a wooden house with the outer walls covered by overlapping long narrow boards.

**physic** ("brand of *physic*")—an old-fashioned term for medicine.

**a den** ("it was a gambling *den*")—a secret meeting-place, where people meet for illegal activities.

**to be up to** ("did not feel her English [was] *up to* the occasion")—(idiom) to be adequate.

**a stake** ("trying to win back his original *stake*")—money risked, an amount placed on a bet.

**to spew** ("began to *spew* out all kinds of people")—to send out in a stream.

**a *kurombo*** (". . . looked at his wife in reproach. "A *kurombo!*' he said.")—(Japanese) a derogatory term for a Negro.

**pomade** ("so unstintingly applied was the *pomade*")—a perfumed cream for the hair and scalp.

**banzai** ("'*banzai,* yippee, *banzai*'")—a Japanese battle cry.

**a lottery** ("'I won it! In the *lottery*'")—an activity whose outcome depends on fate rather than chance or skill, often used to select winners of prizes.

**bleak** ("with such *bleak* eyes")—without hope.

# The Brown House

In California that year the strawberries were marvelous. As large as teacups, they were so juicy and sweet that Mrs. Hattori, making her annual batch of jam, found she could cut down on the sugar considerably. "I suppose this is supposed to be the compensation," she said to her husband, whom she always politely called Mr. Hattori.

"Some compensation!" Mr. Hattori answered.

At that time they were still on the best of terms. It was only later, when the season ended as it had begun, with the market price for strawberries so low nobody bothered to pick number twos, that they began quarreling for the first time in their life together. What provoked the first quarrel and all the rest was that Mr. Hattori, seeing no future in strawberries, began casting around for a way to make some quick cash. Word somehow came to him that there was in a neighboring town a certain house where fortunes were made overnight, and he hurried there at the first opportunity.

It happened that Mrs. Hattori and all the little Hattoris, five of them, all boys and born about a year apart, were with him when he paid his first visit to the house. When he told them to wait in the car, saying he had a little business to transact inside and would return in a trice, he truly meant what he said. He intended only to give the place a brief inspection in order to familiarize himself with it. This was at two o'clock in the afternoon, however, and when he finally made his way back to the car, the day was already so dim that he had to grope around a bit for the door handle.

The house was a large but simple clapboard, recently painted brown and relieved with white window frames. It sat under several enormous eucalyptus trees in the foreground of a few acres of asparagus. To the rear of the house was a ramshackle barn whose spacious blue roof advertised in great yellow letters a ubiquitous brand of physic. Mrs. Hattori, peering toward the house with growing impatience, could not understand what was keeping her husband. She watched other cars either drive into the yard or park along the highway and she saw all sorts of people—white, yellow, brown, and black—

enter the house. Seeing very few people leave, she got the idea
that her husband was attending a meeting or a party.

40      So she was more curious than furious that first time when
Mr. Hattori got around to returning to her and the children. To
her rapid questions Mr. Hattori replied slowly, pensively: it was
a gambling den run by a Chinese family under cover of asparagus, he said, and he had been winning at first, but his luck had
45      suddenly turned, and that was why he had taken so long—he
had been trying to win back his original stake at least.

"How much did you lose?" Mrs. Hattori asked dully.

"Twenty-five dollars," Mr. Hattori said.

"Twenty-five dollars!" exclaimed Mrs. Hattori. "Oh, Mr.
50      Hattori, what have you done?"

At this, as though at a prearranged signal, the baby in her
arms began wailing, and the four boys in the back seat began
complaining of hunger. Mr. Hattori gritted his teeth and drove
on. He told himself that this being assailed on all sides by
55      bawling, whimpering, and murderous glances was no less than
he deserved. Never again, he said to himself; he had learned
his lesson.

Nevertheless, his car, with his wife and children in it, was
parked near the brown house again the following week. This
60      was because he had dreamed a repulsive dream in which a fat
white snake had uncoiled and slithered about and everyone
knows that a white-snake dream is a sure omen of good luck
in games of chance. Even Mrs. Hattori knew this. Besides, she
felt a little guilty about having nagged him so bitterly about the
65      twenty-five dollars. So Mr. Hattori entered the brown house
again on condition that he would return in a half-hour, surely
enough time to test the white snake. When he failed to return
after an hour, Mrs. Hattori sent Joe, the oldest boy, to the front
door to inquire after his father. A Chinese man came to open
70      the door of the grille, looked at Joe, said, "Sorry, no kids in
here," and clacked it to.

When Joe reported back to his mother, she sent him back
again and this time a Chinese woman looked out and said,
"What you want, boy?" When he asked for his father, she asked
75      him to wait, then returned with him to the car, carrying a plate
of Chinese cookies. Joe, munching one thick biscuit as he led
her to the car, found its flavor and texture very strange; it was

unlike either its American or Japanese counterpart so that he could not decide whether he liked it or not.

80     Although the woman was about Mrs. Hattori's age, she immediately called the latter "mama," assuring her that Mr. Hattori would be coming soon, very soon. Mrs. Hattori, mortified, gave excessive thanks for the cookies which she would just as soon have thrown in the woman's face. Mrs. Wu, for so

85     she introduced herself, left them after wagging her head in amazement that Mrs. Hattori, so young, should have so many children and telling her frankly, "No wonder you so skinny, mama."

    "Skinny, ha!" Mrs. Hattori said to the boys. "Well, perhaps.

90     But I'd rather be skinny than fat."

    Joe, looking at the comfortable figure of Mrs. Wu going up the steps of the brown house, agreed.

    Again it was dark when Mr. Hattori came back to the car, but Mrs. Hattori did not say a word. Mr. Hattori made a feeble

95     joke about the unreliability of snakes, but his wife made no attempt to smile. About halfway home she said abruptly, "Please stop the machine, Mr. Hattori. I don't want to ride another inch with you."

    "Now, mother . . ." Mr. Hattori said. "I've learned my lesson.

100     I swear this is the last time."

    "Please stop the machine, Mr. Hattori," his wife repeated.

    Of course the car kept going, so Mrs. Hattori, hugging the baby to herself with one arm, opened the door with her free hand and made as if to hop out of the moving car.

105     The car stopped with a lurch and Mr. Hattori, aghast, said, "Do you want to kill yourself?"

    "That's a very good idea," Mrs. Hattori answered, one leg out of the door.

    "Now, mother . . ." Mr. Hattori said. "I'm sorry; I was wrong

110     to stay so long. I promise on my word of honor never to go near that house again. Come let's go home now and get some supper."

    "Supper!" said Mrs. Hattori. "Do you have any money for groceries?"

115     "I have enough for groceries," Mr. Hattori confessed.

    Mrs. Hattori pulled her leg back in and pulled the door shut. "You see!" she cried triumphantly. "You see!"

The next time, Mrs. Wu brought out besides the cookies a paper sackful of Chinese firecrackers for the boys. "This is
120 America," Mrs. Wu said to Mrs. Hattori. "China and Japan have war, all right, but (she shrugged) it's not our fault. You under-stand?"

Mrs. Hattori nodded, but she did not say anything because she did not feel her English up to the occasion.
125 "Never mind about the firecrackers or the war," she wanted to say. "Just inform Mr. Hattori that his family awaits without."

Suddenly Mrs. Wu, who out of the corner of her eye had been examining another car parked up the street, whispered,
130 "Cops!" and ran back into the house as fast as she could carry her amplitude. Then the windows and doors of the brown house began to spew out all kinds of people—white, yellow, brown, and black—who either got into cars and drove franti-cally away or ran across the street to dive into the field of tall
135 dry weeds. Before Mrs. Hattori and the boys knew what was happening, a Negro man opened the back door of their car and jumped in to crouch at the boys' feet.

The boys, who had never seen such a dark person at close range before, burst into terrified screams, and Mrs. Hattori
140 began yelling too, telling the man to get out, get out. The pant-ing man clasped his hands together and beseeched Mrs. Hattori, "Just let me hide in here until the police go away! I'm asking you to save me from jail!"

Mrs. Hattori made a quick decision. "All right," she said in
145 her tortured English. "Go down, hide!" Then, in Japanese, she assured her sons that this man meant them no harm and ordered them to cease crying, to sit down, to behave, lest she be tempted to give them something to cry about. The policemen had been inside the house about fifteen minutes when Mr. Hat-
150 tori came out. He had been thoroughly frightened, but now he managed to appear jaunty as he told his wife how he had clev-erly thrust all incriminating evidence into a nearby vase of flow-ers and thus escaped arrest. "They searched me and told me I could go," he said. "A lot of others weren't so lucky. One lady
155 fainted."

They were almost a mile from the brown house before the man in back said, "Thanks a million. You can let me off here."

Mr. Hattori was so surprised that the car screeched when it stopped. Mrs. Hattori hastily explained, and the man, paus-

160    ing on his way out, searched for words to emphasize his gratitude. He had always been, he said, a friend of the Japanese people; he knew no race so cleanly, so well-mannered, so downright nice. As he slammed the door shut, he put his hand on the arm of Mr. Hattori, who was still dumfounded, and
165    promised never to forget this act of kindness.

      "What we got to remember," the man said, "is that we all got to die sometime. You might be a king in silk shirts or riding a white horse, but we all got to die sometime."

      Mr. Hattori, starting up the car again, looked at his wife in
170    reproach. "A *kurombo!*" he said. And again, "A *kurombo!*" He pretended to be victim to a shudder.

      "You had no compunctions about that, Mr. Hattori," she reminded him, "when you were inside that house."

      "That's different," Mr. Hattori said.
175    "How so?" Mrs. Hattori inquired.

      The quarrel continued through supper at home, touching on a large variety of subjects. It ended in the presence of the children with Mr. Hattori beating his wife so severely that he had to take her to the doctor to have a few ribs taped. Both in
180    their depths were dazed and shaken that things should have come to such a pass.

      A few weeks after the raid the brown house opened for business as usual, and Mr. Hattori took to going there alone.
185    He no longer waited for weekends but found all sorts of errands to go on during the week which took him in the direction of the asparagus farm. There were nights when he did not bother to come home at all.

      On one such night Mrs. Hattori confided to Joe, because he
190    was the eldest, "Sometimes I lie awake at night and wish for death to overtake me in my sleep. That would be the easiest way." In response Joe wept, principally because he felt tears were expected of him. Mrs. Hattori, deeply moved by his evident commiseration, begged his pardon for burdening his
195    childhood with adult sorrows. Joe was in the first grade that year, and in his sleep he dreamed mostly about school. In one dream that recurred he found himself walking in nakedness and in terrible shame among his closest schoolmates.

      At last Mrs. Hattori could bear it no longer and went away.
200    She took the baby, Sam, and the boy born before him, Ed (for the record, the other two were named Bill and Ogden), to one

of her sisters living in a town about thirty miles distant. Mr. Hattori was shocked and immediately went after her, but her sister refused to let him in the house. "Monster!" this sister said to him from the other side of the door.

Defeated, Mr. Hattori returned home to reform. He worked passionately out in the fields from morning to night, he kept the house spick-and-span, he fed the remaining boys the best food he could buy, and he went out of his way to keep several miles clear of the brown house. This went on for five days, and on the sixth day, one of the Hattoris' nephews, the son of the vindictive lady with whom Mrs. Hattori was taking refuge, came to bring Mr. Hattori a message. The nephew, who was about seventeen at the time, had started smoking cigarettes when he was thirteen. He liked to wear his amorphous hat on the back of his head, exposing a coiffure neatly parted in the middle which looked less like hair than a painted wig, so unstintingly applied was the pomade which held it together. He kept his hands in his pockets, straddled the ground, and let his cigarette dangle to one side of his mouth as he said to Mr. Hattori, "Your wife's taken a powder."

The world actually turned black for an instant for Mr. Hattori as he searched giddily in his mind for another possible interpretation of this ghastly announcement. "Poison?" he queried, a tremor in his knees.

The nephew cackled with restraint. "Nope, you dope," he said. "That means she's leaving your bed and board."

"Talk in Japanese," Mr. Hattori ordered, "and quit trying to be so smart."

Abashed, the nephew took his hands out of his pockets and assisted his meager Japanese with nervous gestures. Mrs. Hattori, he managed to convey, had decided to leave Mr. Hattori permanently and had sent him to get Joe and Bill and Ogden.

"Tell her to go jump in the lake," Mr. Hattori said in English, and in Japanese, "Tell her if she wants the boys, to come back and make a home for them. That's the only way she can ever have them."

Mrs. Hattori came back with Sam and Ed that same night, not only because she had found she was unable to exist without her other sons but because the nephew had glimpsed certain things which indicated that her husband had seen the light. Life for the family became very sweet then because it had lately been so very bitter, and Mr. Hattori went nowhere near the brown house for almost a whole month. When he did resume his visits there, he spaced them frugally and remembered (although this cost him cruel effort) to stay no longer than an hour each time.

One evening Mr. Hattori came home like a madman. He sprinted up the front porch, broke into the house with a bang, and began whirling around the parlor like a human top. Mrs. Hattori dropped her mending and the boys their toys to stare at this phenomenon.

"Yippee," said Mr. Hattori, "banzai, yippee, banzai." Thereupon, he fell dizzily to the floor.

"What is it, Mr. Hattori, are you drunk?" Mrs. Hattori asked, coming to help him up.

"Better than that, mother," Mr. Hattori said, pushing her back to her chair. It was then they noticed that he was holding a brown paper bag in one hand. And from this bag, with the exaggerated ceremony of a magician pulling rabbits from a hat, he began to draw out stack after stack of green bills. These he deposited deliberately, one by one, on Mrs. Hattori's tense lap until the sack was empty and she was buried under a pile of money.

"Explain . . ." Mrs. Hattori gasped.

"I won it! In the lottery! Two thousand dollars! We're rich!" Mr. Hattori explained.

There was a hard silence in the room as everyone looked at the treasure on Mrs. Hattori's lap. Mr. Hattori gazed raptly, the boys blinked in bewilderment, and Mrs. Hattori's eyes bulged a little. Suddenly, without warning, Mrs. Hattori leaped up and vigorously brushed off the front of her clothing, letting the stacks fall where they might. For a moment she clamped her lips together fiercely and glared at her husband. But there was no wisp of steam that curled out from her nostrils and disappeared toward the ceiling; this was just a fleeting illusion that Mr. Hattori had. Then, "You have no conception, Mr. Hattori!" she hissed. "You have absolutely no conception!"

Mr. Hattori was resolute in refusing to burn the money, and Mrs. Hattori eventually adjusted herself to his keeping it. Thus, they increased their property by a new car, a new rug, and their first washing machine. Since these purchases were all

made on the convenient installment plan and the two thousand dollars somehow melted away before they were aware of it,
285 the car and the washing machine were claimed by a collection agency after a few months. The rug remained, however, as it was a fairly cheap one and had already eroded away in spots to show the bare weave beneath. By that time it had become an old habit for Mrs. Hattori and the boys to wait outside the
290 brown house in their original car and for Joe to be commissioned periodically to go to the front door to ask for his father. Joe and his brothers did not mind the long experience too much because they had acquired a taste for Chinese cookies. Nor, really, did Mrs. Hattori, who was pregnant again. After a
295 fashion, she became quite attached to Mrs. Wu who, on her part, decided she had never before encountered a woman with such bleak eyes.

[1951]

## Understanding the Story

1. What is special about the brown house? What circumstances lead Mr. Hattori to go there the first time?

2. After promising himself to "never again" (line 56) visit the gambling den, Mr. Hattori returns the following week. (This a good example of dramatic irony, when a character's action results in the opposite of what he or she had intended.) How does a dream make both Mr. and Mrs. Hattori feel that he should go back to the brown house?

3. How does Mrs. Wu handle Mrs. Hattori's attempts to get her husband to leave the house?

4. In the family's experience with the black man, there are further ironies, particularly verbal irony—a difference between what the speaker and the reader perceive in the situation.

    a. What is the irony of the black man's warm thanks to Mr. Hattori?

b. What is the irony in Mr. Hattori's retort, "That's different" (line 174)?

5. What strategies—verbal, physical, and psychological—does Mrs. Hattori use to encourage her husband to stop gambling? What strategies—verbal, physical, and psychological—does Mr. Hattori use to assert his authority in the family? Who is more successful? Why?

6. In what ways is Joe's reaction to his mother's tears (lines 192–98) different from the nephew's reaction to his aunt and uncle's domestic problems (lines 219–27)? What factors might explain the differences?

7. What are the dramatic ironies (the differences between expectation and result) in Mr. Hattori's winning the lottery and his announcement, "We're rich!" (line 266)?

8. What would explain Mrs. Hattori's "bleak eyes" (line 297)?

9. This story was written with four sections: lines 1–117, 118–181, 182–278, and 279–297. Give each section a title.

## **D**eveloping a Way with Words

1. Identify the character who makes each of the following comments and explain what he or she means by the words in dark type.

    a. "I suppose this is supposed to be **the compensation.**" (lines 4–5)

    b. "China and Japan have war, all right, **but . . . it's not our fault.**" (lines 120–21)

    c. "You might be **a king in silk shirts or riding a white horse,** but **we all got to die sometime.**" (lines 167–68)

    d. "Your wife's **taken a powder.**" (line 221)

    e. "Tell her to **go jump in the lake.**" (line 234)

    f. "**Yippee,** banzai, yippee, banzai." (line 253)

2. At four points in the story, one character has power over another because of greater fluency in a language: Mrs.

Wu over Mrs. Hattori; the black man over Mr. Hattori; the nephew over Mr. Hattori; Mr. Hattori over the nephew.

   a. How does language give power at each of these four points?

   b. From your experience, are the situations realistic?

   (These questions could also provide a topic for writing.)

## M aking Connections

1. Discuss the ways in which "The Brown House" illustrates one or more of the themes mentioned in the introduction. (You might also want to discuss the themes in relation to more recent immigrant groups in the same or other parts of the country.)

   a. How does the brown house provide a context to illustrate the interaction between different ethnic groups in California?

   b. How do the Hattori sons and nephew serve to illustrate the tensions between the first (Isei) and second (Nisei) generations of Japanese Americans?

   c. How do the situations of the adults in the story illustrate the "uneasy adjustment" of the first generation of Japanese Americans?

   d. How does Mrs. Hattori's situation illustrate the special restrictions placed on the first generation of Japanese American women?

2. A stereotype is an unchanging idea, either positive or negative, about something. "The Brown House" provides examples of both positive and negative stereotyping. Discuss, and perhaps write about, one or more of the following questions about racial and ethnic stereotyping.

   a. What is the black man's stereotype of Japanese people? Do you think he would still feel that way if he could hear and understand Mr. Hattori's remarks about him?

b. Do Mr. and Mrs. Hattori seem to be stereotypes of first-generation Japanese immigrants? Why or why not? Do the portraits of Mrs. Wu in "The Brown House" and the old man in "The Chaser" by John Collier seem to be stereotypes of Chinese people? Why or why not?

c. What are the common stereotypes of your ethnic group?

d. Have you ever had the experience of finding that a stereotype you held about another group was inaccurate? What was the experience? What did you learn from it?

3. In both this story and "The Chaser," a man goes into a strange building in search of something. What other similarities are there between the stories? On what points are they different?

4. How do you feel about gambling? Do you know anyone who is a compulsive gambler? Do you approve of legalized gambling? Why or why not?

5. Two of Yamamoto's stories are the basis for the American Playhouse/Public Broadcasting System (PBS) film "Hot Summer Winds" (1991). The film is not presently available for purchase on video cassette; however, teachers in the U.S. may want to contact their local PBS station to ask if the film is on an upcoming program schedule.

# Love

"'A snake is an
enemy to me,' my
father snapped.
'I hate a snake.'"

# Love

*Jesse Stuart*
*(1907–1984)*

Jesse Stuart—a farmer, teacher, and master storyteller—
was born in a log cabin in the foothills of the Appalachian
Mountains in eastern Kentucky, one of the poorest parts of
the United States. Stuart's mother had two years of school-
ing; his father was a coal miner and farmer who never had
the opportunity to learn to read or write. Jesse
Stuart was the first in his family to finish high school, and he
then worked his way through college. But he remained true
to his roots, returning to live on the land where he had been
raised and celebrating his life and the lives of those around
him in fifty-seven books of poetry and prose.

"I am a farmer singing at the plow," Stuart wrote in one
of his early poems. Before that, he had also been a teacher.
It wasn't an easy job, for the Kentucky public school system
paid the lowest wages in the country and the parents were
suspicious of anything to do with education. But the pupils
were eager and Stuart knew from experience that education
was essential to break out of poverty. In a rural high school,
Stuart was expected to teach everything from Latin to algebra, so he often had to work hard to keep ahead of his
pupils. In the third week of Stuart's first year of teaching, a
pupil came to him for help with an algebra problem. Stuart
looked at the problem, then laughed and truthfully said that
he couldn't work it. "Mr. Stuart, I understand," the boy
responded earnestly. "You want your pupils to work these
problems, don't you?" The boy then happily solved the
problem by himself and brought it back. "I knew he was

right after I had seen it worked," Stuart wrote in his autobiographical memoir, *The Thread that Runs So True* (1949). "But Billie Leonard never knew that I couldn't actually work this problem."

To support a wife and family, Stuart had to give up full-time teaching in favor of farming. But he continued writing and in 1937 won a Guggenheim Fellowship that enabled him to spend a year living in Scotland (his ancestral home) and visiting twenty-five other countries. Stuart also taught in poetry and writing programs at several American colleges, and he spent the 1960-61 academic year as a visiting professor of English at the American University in Cairo.

"Love" is characteristic of Stuart's work in being told in the first-person and using the "talk style" of American folklore. Just as urban writers use the names of real streets to provide a sense of reality, so Stuart names specific plants and tools and animals to present the harsh reality and great beauty of an Appalachian hill-country farm. This story also reflects Stuart's love and respect for the hill country and its people, as well as his mountain-man's easy acceptance of death as part of the natural world. Mitch Stuart held the same attitudes, as we see in this passage from *God's Oddling* (1960), Stuart's biography of his father, who also may have provided the idea for "Love":

> "A blacksnake is a pretty thing," he once said to me, "so shiny and black in the spring sun after he sheds his winter skin."
>
> He was the first man I ever heard say a snake was pretty. I never forgot his saying it. I can even remember the sumac thicket where he saw the blacksnake.*

A love story about a snake? Read on.

* From *God's Oddling* (1960), as reprinted in *A Jesse Stuart Reader* (1963).

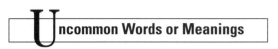

# Uncommon Words or Meanings

**new ground** ("the edge of the *new ground*")—land that hasn't ever been cultivated.

**a cornbalk** ("walked in the *cornbalk*")—rows of planted corn.

**bull** ("a big *bull* blacksnake")—male (animal).

**a copperhead** ("killed twenty-eight *copperheads*")—a poisonous snake.

**a bench** ("at the *bench* of the hill")—a level, narrow stretch of land.

**a greenweed** ("like a *greenweed* held over a new-ground fire")—a small shrub with yellow flowers that shrivels and twists when thrown on a fire.

**a pellet** ("hit against my legs like *pellets*")—a small piece of lead for a shotgun.

**riddled** ("threw her *riddled* body")—filled with holes.

**a quail** ("about the size of a *quail's* egg")—a game bird whose eggs are about one-third the size of a chicken's egg.

**to get up with the chickens** ("This morning my father and I *got up with the chickens.*")—to get up as the sun is rising.

**posthole digger, ax, spud, measuring pole, mattock** ("We got the *posthole digger, ax, spud, measuring pole* and the *mattock.*")—tools used in building a fence.

**I says** ("'Steady,' *I says* to my father.")—a storyteller's shift to "historic present" tense for dramatic emphasis; "I says," suggesting a challenge, is also common in that context.

**to beat** ("'Did you ever see anything to *beat* that?'")—(informal) to excel or surpass.

# Love

Yesterday when the bright sun blazed down on the wilted corn my father and I walked around the edge of the new ground to plan a fence. The cows kept coming through the chestnut oaks on the cliff and running over the young corn. They bit off
5 the tips of the corn and trampled down the stubble.

My father walked in the cornbalk. Bob, our Collie, walked in front of my father. We heard a ground squirrel whistle down over the bluff among the dead treetops at the clearing's edge. "Whoop, take him, Bob," said my father. He lifted up a young
10 stalk of corn, with wilted dried roots, where the ground squirrel had dug it up for the sweet grain of corn left on its tender roots. This has been a dry spring and the corn has kept well in the earth where the grain has sprouted. The ground squirrels love this corn. They dig up rows of it and eat the sweet grains. The
15 young corn stalks are killed and we have to replant the corn.

I could see my father keep sicking Bob after the ground squirrel. He jumped over the corn rows. He started to run toward the ground squirrel. I, too, started running toward the clearing's edge where Bob was jumping and barking. The dust
20 flew in tiny swirls behind our feet. There was a big cloud of dust behind us.

"It's a big bull blacksnake," said my father. "Kill him, Bob! Kill him, Bob!"

Bob was jumping and snapping at the snake so as to make
25 it strike and throw itself off guard. Bob has killed twenty-eight copperheads this spring. He knows how to kill a snake. He doesn't rush to do it. He takes his time and does the job well.

"Let's don't kill the snake," I said. "A blacksnake is a harmless snake. It kills poison snakes. It kills the copperhead. It
30 catches more mice from the fields than a cat."

I could see the snake didn't want to fight the dog. The snake wanted to get away. Bob wouldn't let it. I wondered why it was crawling toward a heap of black loamy earth at the bench of the hill. I wondered why it had come from the chest-
35 nut oak sprouts and the matted greenbriars on the cliff. I looked as the snake lifted its pretty head in response to one of

Bob's jumps. "It's not a bull blacksnake," I said. "It's a she-snake. Look at the white on her throat."

"A snake is an enemy to me," my father snapped. "I hate a
40  snake. Kill it, Bob. Go in there and get that snake and quit play-ing with it!"

Bob obeyed my father. I hated to see him take this snake by the throat. She was so beautifully poised in the sunlight. Bob grabbed the white patch on her throat. He cracked her
45  long body like an ox whip in the wind. He cracked it against the wind only. The blood spurted from her fine-curved throat. Something hit against my legs like pellets. Bob threw the snake down. I looked to see what had struck my legs. It was snake eggs. Bob had slung them from her body. She was going
50  to the sand heap to lay her eggs, where the sun is the setting-hen that warms them and hatches them.

Bob grabbed her body there on the earth where the red blood was running down on the gray-piled loam. Her body was still writing in pain. She acted like a greenweed held over a
55  new-ground fire. Bob slung her viciously many times. He cracked her limp body against the wind. She was now limber as a shoestring in the wind. Bob threw her riddled body back on the sand. She quivered like a leaf in the lazy wind, then her riddled body lay perfectly still. The blood covered the loamy
60  earth around the snake.

"Look at the eggs, won't you?" said my father. We counted thirty-seven eggs. I picked an egg up and held it in my hand. Only a minute ago there was life in it. It was an immature seed. It would not hatch. Mother sun could not incubate it on the
65  warm earth. The egg I held in my hand was almost the size of a quail's egg. The shell on it was thin and tough and the egg appeared under the surface to be a watery egg.

"Well, Bob, I guess you see now why this snake couldn't fight," I said. "It is life. Stronger devour the weaker even
70  among human beings. Dog kills snake. Snake kills birds. Birds kill the butterflies. Man conquers all. Man, too, kills for sport."

Bob was panting. He walked ahead of us back to the house. His tongue was out of his mouth. He was tired. He was hot under his shaggy coat of hair. His tongue nearly touched
75  the dry dirt and white flecks of foam dripped from it. We walked toward the house. Neither my father nor I spoke. I still thought of the dead snake. The sun was going down over the

chestnut ridge. A lark was singing. It was late for a lark to sing. The red evening clouds floated above the pine trees on our
80   pasture hill. My father stood beside the path. His black hair was moved by the wind. His face was red in the blue wind of day. His eyes looked toward the sinking sun.

"And my father hates a snake," I thought.

I thought about the agony women know of giving birth. I
85   thought about how they will fight to save their children. Then, I thought of the snake. I thought it was silly of me to think such thoughts.

This morning my father and I got up with the chickens. He says one has to get up with the chickens to do a day's work. We
90   got the posthole digger, ax, spud, measuring pole and the mattock. We started for the clearing's edge. Bob didn't go along.

The dew was on the corn. My father walked behind with the posthole digger across his shoulder. I walked in front. The wind was blowing. It was a good morning wind to breathe and
95   a wind that makes one feel like he can get under the edge of a hill and heave the whole hill upside down.

I walked out the corn row where we had come yesterday afternoon. I looked in front of me. I saw something. I saw it move. It was moving like a huge black rope winds around a
100   windlass. "Steady," I says to my father. "Here is the bull blacksnake." He took one step up beside me and stood. His eyes grew wide apart.

"What do you know about this," he said.

"You have seen the bull blacksnake now," I said. "Take a
105   good look at him! He is lying beside his dead mate. He has come to her. He, perhaps, was on her trail yesterday."

The male snake had trailed her to her doom. He had come in the night, under the roof of stars, as the moon shed rays of light on the quivering clouds of green. He had found his lover
110   dead. He was coiled beside her, and she was dead.

The bull blacksnake lifted his head and followed us as we walked around the dead snake. He would have fought us to his death. He would have fought Bob to his death. "Take a stick," said my father, "and throw him over the hill so Bob won't find
115   him. Did to you ever see anything to beat that? I've heard they'd do that. But this is my first time to see it." I took a stick and threw him over the bank into the dewy sprouts on the cliff.

[1940]

## U̲nderstanding the Story

1. Why was it important for the young man (the narrator) and his father to put a fence around their land? How was their dog, Bob, helping them? Why does the narrator refer to the dog as "he" rather than "it"?

2. Why was it important to kill ground squirrels? What about snakes? What explains why the snake wasn't willing to fight the dog (line 31)?

3. When does the narrator begin to refer to the snake as "she" instead of "it"? Are you surprised to find a snake described (line 36) as having a "pretty" head? What other complimentary descriptions of the she-snake are there?

4. How do the following similes (a direct comparison with *like* or *as*) help the reader to picture the dog killing the snake? How are the comparisons appropriate to the setting of the story?

    a. He cracked her long body like an ox whip in the wind. (lines 44–45)

    b. Something hit against my legs like pellets. (line 47)

    c. She was now limber as a shoestring in the wind. (lines 56–57)

    d. She quivered like a leaf in the lazy wind . . . . (line 58)

5. When the narrator says "It is life" (line 69), what does "it" refer to? How are the setting sun and "red evening clouds" (line 79) appropriate to the event that has just taken place?

6. What thoughts does the narrator dismiss as "silly" (line 86)? Why does he see them that way? Do you agree? Do you think the author agrees?

7. In the first of the following sentences, what pronoun and what simile are used in describing the snake? In the

second and third sentences, how have the pronoun and the imagery changed? How do those changes affect the reader's feelings about the snake?

    a. It was moving like a huge black rope winds around a windlass. (lines 99–100)

    b. "He is lying beside his dead mate." (line 105)

    c. The male snake had trailed her to her doom. He had come in the night, under the roof of stars, as the moon shed rays of light on the quivering clouds of green. He had found his lover dead. He was coiled beside her, and she was dead. (lines 107–110)

8. In the final paragraph, what shows that the father has changed his mind about every snake being "an enemy," as he had said earlier (line 39)? What has caused him to change his view?

## Developing a Way with Words

1. This story is filled with images of birth—for example, "It was snake *eggs*." (lines 48–49)—and death—for example, "*dead treetops* at the clearing's edge" (line 8). How many more of each can you find? What effect do they have on the story as a whole?

2. In his poetry, Stuart often celebrates the Kentucky spring. Discuss the image he creates in the following description (lines 93–96): "The wind was blowing. It was a good morning wind to breathe and a wind that makes one feel like he can get under the edge of a hill and heave the whole hill upside down." Have you known days that made you feel like that?

## Making Connections

1. What happens to each of the characters as a result of the events that take place? In this story, does "characters"

refer only to humans or does it include the dog and the snakes as well?

2. What statement about love and hate is Stuart making? How, from the evidence in this story, does each affect people?

3. How does Stuart's view of romantic love differ from Collier's view in "The Chaser"? What experience have you had—or do you know of—that represents your idea of true love?

4. In this story, Stuart suggests that parents can make mistakes and that it's hard for an older person to admit a mistake to a younger one. In this story, what mistake did the father make? How did he show his regret? Have you had a similar experience in your own life? If so, what kind of mistake did the older person make? How, if at all, did he or she admit the mistake?

5. In "Love," the father is a farmer who sees all snakes as enemies. In "The Brown House" by Hisaye Yamamoto, the Hattoris are also farmers, but they believe that a white snake in a dream means good luck. How common are those contrasting ideas about snakes in American and Japanese culture today? Ask several people who were raised in the American culture and several people who were raised in the Japanese culture how they feel about snakes. Then report how your findings do or do not reflect these stories.

6. Three other stories in this book—"The Unicorn in the Garden" by James Thurber, "The Summer of the Beautiful White Horse" by William Saroyan, and "A Blizzard Under Blue Sky" by Pam Houston—have animals as important characters. What other stories do you know—in books, movies, or real life—that have animals as main characters? What are the animals like in those stories? Do any of the stories deal with a love relationship between animals? For a writing assignment, compare and contrast the use of animals as characters in this story and the Thurber, Saroyan, or Houston story.

# The Use of Force

"... it was up to

me to tell them;

that's why they

were spending

three dollars

on me."

# The Use of Force

## William Carlos Williams
## (1883–1963)

William Carlos Williams was born and raised in Rutherford, New Jersey. He was the son of an international marriage—his father was an Englishman who traveled in Europe and Latin America as a sales representative for an American drug company; his mother came from a well-to-do Puerto Rican family. Williams attended preparatory schools in New York and Switzerland, then studied to become a doctor, like his mother's brother Carlos, for whom he was named. After graduating from the University of Pennsylvania Medical School, Williams returned to his hometown as a school doctor and general practitioner. In that capacity, Williams held office hours in the morning and evening; in the afternoon, he visited schools and made house calls to see sick patients. When Williams went to Leipzig, Germany, to study for the new specialty in pediatrics (the medical care of infants and children), he joked that he was specializing to cut down on his practice.

While working more than full-time as a school and family doctor, Williams was also becoming one of the most prolific of twentieth-century American authors. He published his first volume of poems at the age of twenty-three, and in his lifetime published six hundred poems, fifty-two short stories, four novels, an opera libretto, and *The Autobiography of William Carlos Williams* (1951), as well as other non-fiction works. He found the energy to do his writing at night and at odd moments during the day, explaining that in concentrating on his patients' illnesses he "became *them*," allowing his own self to rest. "For the moment, I myself did not exist. Nothing of myself affected me. As a consequence, I came back to myself, as from any other sleep, rested."

"The Use of Force" is one of Williams' thirteen stories based directly on his experiences as a small town doctor, visiting a family that he hasn't met before.* The family doesn't have much money (the kitchen is the only room in the house that is heated) and they are suspicious of doctors. Yet they fear that their daughter may have diphtheria, which has already been diagnosed in other children in her school. In the 1930s, when the story first appeared, readers would have recognized the signs and danger of that highly contagious disease. Diphtheria normally begins with a coating of membrane in the throat. While some forms of the disease are mild, most are severe and can result in heart failure in as little as three days.

The story forcefully exemplifies Williams' comment in his *Autobiography* that "though I might be attracted or repelled, the professional attitude which every physician must call on would steady me, dictate the terms on which I was to proceed." The doctor in the story is steady in his approach. Yet in the *Autobiography,* Williams continues: "Many a time a man must watch the patient's mind as it watches him, distrusting him, . . . ." In "The Use of Force," he shows what the challenge of a strong patient's distrust may trigger in a doctor, who is, after all, a human being like any other.

*These stories, together with six doctor-related poems and a description of his practice from Williams' *Autobiography,* have been collected by Robert Coles in *William Carlos Williams: The Doctor Stories* (1984).

## Uncommon Words or Meanings

**to eye (someone) up and down** ("*eyeing* me *up and down* distrustfully")—(idiom) to look at (someone) carefully from head to foot.

**to be up to (someone)** ("it *was up to* me to tell them")—to be (someone's) responsibility.

**photogravure** ("the *photogravure* sections of the Sunday paper")—a printing process for reproducing pictures in color, recently invented at the time of the story.

**tho't** ("we *tho't* you'd better look her over")—"thought."

**to look (someone) over** ("we tho't you'd better *look* her *over*")—to examine.

**to take a trial shot** ("I *took a trial shot* at it")—(idiom) to make a first attempt at something.

**a point of departure** ("I took a trial shot at it as a *point of departure*")—a starting point, here for a diagnosis.

**Nothing doing** (". . . let's take a look at your throat. *Nothing doing.*")—(informal) a flat refusal; a firm "no."

**aw** ("*Aw*, come on, I coaxed")—an interjection, here used to be persuasive.

**ground** ("At that I *ground* my teeth in disgust.")—past tense of **grind,** to rub together with great pressure.

**a culture** ("I had to have a throat *culture* for her own protection.")—a sample of tissue to be examined for infection.

**Oh yeah** ("*Oh yeah?* I had to smile to myself.")—(idiom) casual pronunciation of "Oh, yes?" to show disbelief in what has just been said.

**abject** ("they grew more and more *abject,* crushed, and exhausted")—deserving contempt.

**bred** ("insane fury of effort *bred* of her terror of me")—past participle of **breed,** to be caused or produced by (something).

**an operative** ("a blind fury, a feeling of adult shame . . . are the *operatives*")—an essential factor in causing an action.

**to gag** ("down her throat till she *gagged*")—to choke because the throat is closing involuntarily.

# The Use of Force

They were new patients to me, all I had was the name, Olson. Please come down as soon as you can, my daughter is very sick.

When I arrived I was met by the mother, a big startled looking woman, very clean and apologetic who merely said, Is this the doctor? and let me in. In the back, she added. You must excuse us, doctor, we have her in the kitchen where it is warm. It is very damp here sometimes.

The child was fully dressed and sitting on her father's lap near the kitchen table. He tried to get up, but I motioned for him not to bother, took off my overcoat and started to look things over. I could see that they were all very nervous, eyeing me up and down distrustfully. As often, in such cases, they weren't telling me more than they had to, it was up to me to tell them; that's why they were spending three dollars on me.

The child was fairly eating me up with her cold, steady eyes, and no expression to her face whatever. She did not move and seemed, inwardly, quiet; an unusually attractive little thing, and as strong as a heifer in appearance. But her face was flushed, she was breathing rapidly, and I realized that she had a high fever. She had magnificent blond hair, in profusion. One of those picture children often reproduced in advertising leaflets and the photogravure sections of the Sunday papers.

She's had a fever for three days, began the father and we don't know what it comes from. My wife has given her things, you know, like people do, but it don't do no good. And there's been a lot of sickness around. So we tho't you'd better look her over and tell us what is the matter.

As doctors often do I took a trial shot at it as a point of departure. Has she had a sore throat?

Both parents answered me together, No . . . No, she says her throat don't hurt her.

Does your throat hurt you? added the mother to the child. But the little girl's expression didn't change nor did she move her eyes from my face.

Have you looked?

I tried to, said the mother, but I couldn't see.

As it happens we had been having a number of cases of diphtheria in the school to which this child went during that
40 month and we were all, quite apparently, thinking of that, though no one had as yet spoken of the thing.

Well, I said, suppose we take a look at the throat first. I smiled in my best professional manner and asking for the child's first name I said, come on, Mathilda, open your mouth
45 and let's take a look at your throat.

Nothing doing.

Aw, come on, I coaxed, just open your mouth wide and let me take a look. Look, I said, opening both hands wide, I haven't anything in my hands. Just open up and let me see.

50 Such a nice man, put in the mother. Look how kind he is to you. Come on, do what he tells you to. He won't hurt you.

At that I ground my teeth in disgust. If only they wouldn't use the word "hurt" I might be able to get somewhere. But I did not allow myself to be hurried or disturbed but speaking qui-
55 etly and slowly I approached the child again.

As I moved my chair a little nearer suddenly with one cat-like movement both her hands clawed instinctively for my eyes and she almost reached them too. In fact she knocked my glasses flying and they fell, though unbroken, several feet
60 away from me on the kitchen floor.

Both the mother and father almost turned themselves inside out in embarrassment and apology. You bad girl, said the mother, taking her and shaking her by one arm. Look what you've done. The nice man . . .

65 For heaven's sake, I broke in. Don't call me a nice man to her. I'm here to look at her throat on the chance that she might have diphtheria and possibly die of it. But that's nothing to her. Look here, I said to the child, we're going to look at your throat. You're old enough to understand what I'm saying. Will you open
70 it now by yourself or shall we have to open it for you?

Not a move. Even her expression hadn't changed. Her breaths however were coming faster and faster. Then the bat-tle began. I had to do it. I had to have a throat culture for her own protection. But first I told the parents that it was entirely
75 up to them. I explained the danger but said that I would not insist on a throat examination so long as they would take the responsibility.

If you don't do what the doctor says you'll have to go to the hospital, the mother admonished her severely.

Oh yeah? I had to smile to myself. After all, I had already fallen in love with the savage brat, the parents were contemptible to me. In the ensuing struggle they grew more and more abject, crushed, and exhausted while she surely rose to magnificent heights of insane fury of effort bred of her terror of me.

The father tried his best, and he was a big man but the fact that she was his daughter, his shame at her behavior and his dread of hurting her made him release her just at the critical moment several times when I had almost achieved success, till I wanted to kill him. But his dread also that she might have diphtheria made him tell me to go on, go on though he himself was almost fainting, while the mother moved back and forth behind us raising and lowering her hands in an agony of apprehension.

Put her in front of you on your lap, I ordered, and hold both her wrists.

But as soon as he did the child let out a scream. Don't, you're hurting me. Let go of my hands. Let them go I tell you. Then she shrieked terrifyingly, hysterically. Stop it! Stop it! You're killing me!

Do you think she can stand it, doctor! said the mother.

You get out, said the husband to his wife. Do you want her to die of diphtheria?

Come on now, hold her, I said.

Then I grasped the child's head with my left hand and tried to get the wooden tongue depressor between her teeth. She fought, with clenched teeth, desperately! But now I also had grown furious—at a child. I tried to hold myself down but I couldn't. I know how to expose a throat for inspection. And I did my best. When finally I got the wooden spatula behind the last teeth and just the point of it into the mouth cavity, she opened up for an instant but before I could see anything she came down again and gripping the wooden blade between her molars she reduced it to splinters before I could get it out again.

Aren't you ashamed, the mother yelled at her. Aren't you ashamed to act like that in front of the doctor?

Get me a smooth-handled spoon of some sort, I told the mother. We're going through with this. The child's mouth was already bleeding. Her tongue was cut and she was screaming in wild hysterical shrieks. Perhaps I should have desisted and come back in an hour or more. No doubt it would have been better. But I have seen at least two children lying dead in bed of neglect in such cases, and feeling that I must get a diagnosis now or never I went at it again. But the worst of it was that I too had got beyond reason. I could have torn the child apart in my own fury and enjoyed it. It was a pleasure to attack her. My face was burning with it.

The damned little brat must be protected against her own idiocy, one says to oneself at such times. Others must be protected against her. It is a social necessity. And all these things are true. But a blind fury, a feeling of adult shame, bred of a longing for muscular release are the operatives. One goes on to the end.

In a final unreasoning assault I overpowered the child's neck and jaws. I forced the heavy silver spoon back of her teeth and down her throat till she gagged. And there it was—both tonsils covered with membrane. She had fought valiantly to keep me from knowing her secret. She had been hiding that sore throat for three days at least and lying to her parents in order to escape just such an outcome as this.

Now truly she *was* furious. She had been on the defensive before but now she attacked. Tried to get off her father's lap and fly at me while tears of defeat blinded her eyes.

[1938]

## Understanding the Story

1. What does the reader know about the parents from the description of them in the first three paragraphs? In what way or ways is the daughter different from her parents?

2. Why is it important for the doctor to see the girl's throat? In what different ways does the doctor tell us about the medical danger?

3. How do the doctor, the father, and the mother each try to get the girl to cooperate? How do their approaches

conflict? Why do all of the approaches fail? (What does Mathilda fear? What do her parents fear?)

4. Doctors are usually thought of as being emotionally neutral toward their patients. But the doctor in this story is certainly not neutral when he says (lines 80–83), "I had already fallen in love with the savage brat, the parents were contemptible to me." What accounts for his very different feelings about Mathilda and her parents?

5. When the doctor forces the girl's mouth open, he says (lines 123–124), "But the worst of it was that I, too, had got beyond reason."

   a. What does it mean to be "beyond reason"?

   b. "I, too" suggests that at least one other person was "beyond reason." Who?

   c. In the course of the story, what are the stages in the doctor's change from feeling calm and in control to feeling barely controlled fury?

6. What were the logical reasons for doing whatever was necessary to examine the girl's throat right away? What were the non-logical—the emotional or instinctive—reasons?

7. Is it a surprise that, in the end, the girl proves to have diphtheria? Why or why not?

## Developing a Way with Words

1. In the story, there are many references to looking, seeing, not wanting to see, and trying to prevent seeing. In the following sentences from the story, what kind of looking or seeing does each of the phrases in dark type describe? What other references to looking and seeing are there in the story? (This question could also be used for discussion and writing.)

   a. I . . . took off my overcoat and started to **look things over.** I could **see** that they were all very nervous, **eyeing me up and down** distrustfully. (lines 10–13)

b. **Have you looked?**
I tried to, said the mother, but I **couldn't see.** (line 36)

c. . . . just open your mouth wide and let me **take a look.
Look,** I said, opening both hands wide, I haven't anything in my hands. Just open up and **let me see.** (lines
47–49)

d. . . . clawed instinctively for **my eyes** and she almost
reached them too. In fact she knocked **my glasses** flying . . . . (lines 57–59)

e. . . . a **blind** fury . . . . (line 130)

f. . . . tears of defeat **blinded her eyes.** (line 142)

2. When someone's exact words are used in a story, the
convention is to put the words in quotation marks. This
story contains a good deal of such direct speech, yet
there are no quotation marks. Choose a paragraph with
direct speech and add the standard punctuation.

How does that change the "feeling" of the paragraph?
Why do you think Williams chose to ignore the convention of quotation marks?

# Making Connections

1. What does each character in the story fear? Which of
them do you feel the most sympathy for? Why?

2. The story is told from the doctor's point of view. How
would the story have been different if the mother were
the narrator? the father? the girl?

3. Why do you think Mathilda had, as the doctor said,
"fought valiantly" (line 136) to keep anyone from knowing that she was ill? Why do people sometimes try to
conceal symptoms from others who care about them?
Have you ever known anyone who concealed a serious
illness or done that yourself? If so, what was the result?

4. Are you surprised that Williams tells us so much about a doctor's personal feeling? Do you think that his medical experience and feelings, as reflected in this story, are unusual? Why or why not?

5. Consider these facts about the disease of diphtheria: It is a highly contagious disease caused by airborne bacteria. Before inoculations were available, it often spread rapidly through a community. The first symptoms, a fever and sore throat, are the same for many diseases. A more serious symptom, membrane growing in the throat, isn't visible without a specific examination. A severe case may result in death in as little as three days. Williams has used diphtheria as a metaphor (an implied comparison) for the "disease" of the unreasoning anger and violence that are released by using force against a weaker opponent. Is the metaphor appropriate? Why or why not?

6. When the English statesman Edmund Burke argued in the British Parliament, in March 1775, against declaring war on the thirteen American colonies, he said: "The use of force alone is but *temporary.* It may subdue for a moment; but it does not remove the necessity of subduing again: and a nation is not governed, which is perpetually to be conquered." Do you think that Burke would feel that the doctor has "won" something through the use of force? Would Burke believe that Mathilda's spirit has been broken by the doctor's use of force? Why or why not?

# The Lottery

"Bobby Martin

had already

stuffed his

pockets full of

stones, . . . ."

# The Lottery

## Shirley Jackson
## (1919–1965)

For most of her life (she died in her sleep at the age of forty-eight), Shirley Jackson felt like an outsider. As a child in San Francisco, she felt that her glamorous, socially ambitious mother was disappointed to have a plain, awkward daughter. As an adult married to a brilliant literary critic who taught at an expensive woman's college in Vermont, Jackson felt that her husband's colleagues and students saw her only as a plain, overweight faculty wife. She also felt that the townspeople of North Bennington, where they lived, regarded her as an outsider on many counts—she was from California, she was a woman writer, she was married to a New York Jewish intellectual, and they were associated with the college. Increasing her sense of "otherness" was Jackson's deep interest in witchcraft and her belief that she had supernatural powers.

Shirley Jackson also had a good mind, a quick sense of humor, and a great gift for writing. She turned her experiences in raising four lively children into humorous short stories, among them "Charles" (1948), and novels such as *Life Among the Savages* (1953). Jackson turned her fears of the outside world into chilling works of fiction, including the novel *We Have Always Lived in the Castle* (1962) and her most famous work, "The Lottery" (1948). The story came to her, she later said, one spring day on her way home from the morning grocery shopping. She was moving slowly because in addition to being four months pregnant, Jackson was pushing her two-year-old up the steep hill in a stroller while carrying two bags of groceries. But when she got home, she rapidly put away the groceries, settled the baby in the playpen, and sat down to write the story. By the time her five-year-old came home for lunch, the story was done. Jackson made a few minor changes that evening, then mailed the story to her literary agent in New York. *The New Yorker* quickly accepted it, asking only that the date of the lottery be made to coincide with the date of the issue in which it would appear—June 27.*

The story is set in a small New England farming community. As in North Bennington, a town common (common grazing land in Colonial times) is used for civic gatherings. Every year the townspeople hold a lottery—an activity in which people randomly draw "lots" to determine a winner. What do you suppose the prize will be? The setting and characters in the story seem realistic but the action, rather than being a factual report of a real event, is a portrayal of human nature. What aspects of human nature do you suppose it will show?

Evidently many readers recognize a part of themselves that they would rather not see. "The Lottery" brought the largest volume of mail that *The New Yorker* had ever received on a story, as well as puzzled and angry letters to Jackson's home—more than three hundred letters in all. Subsequently "The Lottery" has been dramatized for radio and TV, has been the subject of a ballet, and is regularly reprinted in anthologies. It is a story that a reader never forgets.

* Jackson recounts this in "Biography of a Story," a lecture reprinted in her posthumous collection *Come Along with Me,* edited by her husband, Stanley Edgar Hyman (1968). A carefully-documented and sympathetic treatment of Jackson's life can be found in Judy Oppenheimer, *Private Demons: The Life of Shirley Jackson* (1988).

## Uncommon Words or Meanings

**a house dress** ("faded *house dresses*")—an inexpensive cotton dress worn for working at home.

**a recital** ("a *recital* of some sort")—something said aloud from memory; a recitation.

**a chant** ("tuneless *chant*")—a monotonous, rhythmic recitation.

**to lapse** ("this part . . . had been allowed to *lapse*")—to pass away by neglect.

**(someone's) old man** ("'Thought my *old man* was out back'")—(informal) husband.

**Missus** ("'Here comes your *Missus,* Hutchinson.'")—(informal) wife.

**stoutly** ("said *stoutly*")—with determination.

**a good sport** ("'Be a *good sport,* Tessie'")—(idiom) someone who plays (a game) fairly and is willing to accept defeat without complaining.

# The Lottery

The morning of June 27th was clear and sunny, with the fresh warmth of a full-summer day; the flowers were blossoming profusely and the grass was richly green. The people of the village began to gather in the square, between the post office and the bank, around ten o'clock; in some towns there were so many people that the lottery took two days and had to be started on June 26th, but in this village, where there were only about three hundred people, the whole lottery took less than two hours, so it could begin at ten o'clock in the morning and still be through in time to allow the villagers to get home for noon dinner.

The children assembled first, of course. School was recently over for the summer, and the feeling of liberty sat uneasily on most of them; they tended to gather together quietly for a while before they broke into boisterous play, and their talk was still of the classroom and the teacher, of books and reprimands. Bobby Martin had already stuffed his pockets full of stones, and the other boys soon followed his example, selecting the smoothest and roundest stones; Bobby and Harry Jones and Dicky Delacroix—the villagers pronounced this name "Dellacroy"—eventually made a great pile of stones in one corner of the square and guarded it against the raids of the other boys. The girls stood aside, talking among themselves, looking over their shoulders at the boys, and the very small children rolled in the dust or clung to the hands of their older brothers or sisters.

Soon the men began to gather, surveying their children, speaking of planting and rain, tractors and taxes. They stood together, away from the pile of stones in the corner, and their jokes were quiet and they smiled rather than laughed. The women, wearing faded house dresses and sweaters, came shortly after their menfolk. They greeted one another and exchanged bits of gossip as they went to join their husbands. Soon the women, standing by their husbands, began to call their children, and the children came reluctantly, having to be called four or five times. Bobby Martin ducked under his mother's grasping hand and ran, laughing, back to the pile of stones. His father spoke up sharply, and Bobby came quickly and took his place between his father and his oldest brother.

The lottery was conducted—as were the square dances, the teen-age club, the Halloween program—by Mr. Summers, who had time and energy to devote to civic activities. He was a round-faced jovial man and he ran the coal business, and people were sorry for him, because he had no children and his wife was a scold. When he arrived in the square, carrying the black wooden box, there was a murmur of conversation among the villagers, and he waved and called, "Little late today, folks." The postmaster, Mr. Graves, followed him, carrying a three-legged stool, and the stool was put in the center of the square and Mr. Summers set the black box down on it. The villagers kept their distance, leaving a space between them and the stool, and when Mr. Summers said, "Some of you fellows want to give me a hand?" there was a hesitation before two men, Mr. Martin and his oldest son, Baxter, came forward to hold the box steady on the stool while Mr. Summers stirred up the papers inside.

The original paraphernalia for the lottery had been lost long ago, and the black box now resting on the stool had been put into use even before Old Man Warner, the oldest man in town, was born. Mr. Summers spoke frequently to the villagers about making a new box, but no one liked to upset even as much tradition as was represented by the black box. There was a story that the present box had been made with some pieces from the box that had preceded it, the one that had been constructed when the first people settled down to make a village here. Every year, after the lottery, Mr. Summers began talking again about a new box, but every year the subject was allowed to fade off without anything's being done. The black box grew shabbier each year; by now it was no longer completely black but splintered badly along one side to show the original wood color, and in some places faded or stained.

Mr. Martin and his oldest son, Baxter, held the black box securely on the stool until Mr. Summers had stirred the papers thoroughly with his hand. Because so much of the ritual had been forgotten or discarded, Mr. Summers had been successful in having slips of paper substituted for the chips of wood that had been used for generations. Chips of wood, Mr. Summers had argued, had been all very well when the village was tiny, but now that the population was more than three hundred and likely to keep growing, it was necessary to use something that would fit more easily into the black box. The night before the lottery, Mr. Summers and Mr. Graves made up the slips of paper and put them in the box, and it was then taken to the safe of Mr. Summers' coal company and locked up until Mr. Summers was ready to take it to the square the next morning. The rest of the year, the box was put away, sometimes one place, sometimes another; it had spent one year in Mr. Graves' barn and another year underfoot in the post office, and sometimes it was set on a shelf in the Martin grocery and left there.

There was a great deal of fussing to be done before Mr. Summers declared the lottery open. There were the lists to make up—of heads of families, heads of households in each family, members of each household in each family. There was the proper swearing-in of Mr. Summers by the postmaster, as the official of the lottery; at one time, some people remembered, there had been a recital of some sort, performed by the official of the lottery, a perfunctory, tuneless chant that had been rattled off duly each year; some people believed that the official of the lottery used to stand just so when he said or sang it, others believed that he was supposed to walk among the people, but years and years ago this part of the ritual had been allowed to lapse. There had been, also, a ritual salute, which the official of the lottery had had to use in addressing each person who came up to draw from the box, but this also had changed with time, until now it was felt necessary only for the official to speak to each person approaching. Mr. Summers was very good at all this; in his clean white shirt and blue jeans, with one hand resting carelessly on the black box, he seemed very proper and important as he talked interminably to Mr. Graves and the Martins.

Just as Mr. Summers finally left off talking and turned to the assembled villagers, Mrs. Hutchinson came hurriedly along the path to the square, her sweater thrown over her shoulders, and slid into place at the back of the crowd. "Clean forgot what day it was," she said to Mrs. Delacroix, who stood next to her, and they both laughed softly. "Thought my old man was out back stacking wood," Mrs. Hutchinson went on, "and then I looked and the kids was gone and then I remembered it was the twenty-seventh and came a-running." She dried her hands on her apron, and Mrs. Delacroix said, "You're in time, though. They're still talking away up there."

Mrs. Hutchinson craned her neck to see through the crowd and found her husband and children standing near the front. She tapped Mrs. Delacroix on the arm as a farewell and began to make her way through the crowd. The people separated good-humoredly to let her through; two or three people said, in voices just loud enough to be heard across the crowd, "Here comes your Missus, Hutchinson," and "Bill, she made it after all." Mrs. Hutchinson reached her husband, and Mr. Summers, who had been waiting, said cheerfully, "Thought we were going to have to get on without you, Tessie." Mrs. Hutchinson said, grinning, "Wouldn't have me leave m'dishes in the sink, now, would you, Joe?" and soft laughter ran through the crowd as the people stirred back into position after Mrs. Hutchinson's arrival.

"Well, now," Mr. Summers said soberly, "guess we better get started, get this over with, so's we can go back to work. Anybody ain't here?"

"Dunbar," several people said. "Dunbar, Dunbar."

Mr. Summers consulted his list. "Clyde Dunbar," he said. "That's right. He's broke his leg, hasn't he? Who's drawing for him?"

"Me, I guess," a woman said, and Mr. Summers turned to look at her. "Wife draws for her husband," Mr. Summers said. "Don't you have a grown boy to do it for you, Janey?" Although Mr. Summers and everyone else in the village knew the answer perfectly well, it was the business of the official of the lottery to ask such questions formally. Mr. Summers waited with an expression of polite interest while Mrs. Dunbar answered.

"Horace's not but sixteen yet," Mrs. Dunbar said regretfully. "Guess I gotta fill in for the old man this year."

"Right," Mr. Summers said. He made a note on the list he was holding. Then he asked, "Watson boy drawing this year?"

A tall boy in the crowd raised his hand. "Here," he said. "I'm drawing for m'mother and me." He blinked his eyes nervously and ducked his head as several voices in the crowd said things like "Good fellow, Jack," and "Glad to see your mother's got a man to do it."

"Well," Mr. Summers said, "guess that's everyone. Old Man Warner make it?" "Here," a voice said, and Mr. Summers nodded.

* * *

A sudden hush fell on the crowd as Mr. Summers cleared
his throat and looked at the list. "All ready?" he called. "Now,
I'll read the names of heads of families first and the men come
up and take a paper out of the box. Keep the paper folded in
your hand without looking at it until everyone has had a turn,
everything clear?"

The people had done it so many times that they only half
listened to the directions; most of them were quiet, wetting
their lips, not looking around. Then Mr. Summers raised one
hand high and said, "Adams." A man disengaged himself from
the crowd and came forward. "Hi, Steve," Mr. Summers said,
and Mr. Adams said, "Hi, Joe." They grinned at one another
humorlessly and nervously. Then Mr. Adams reached into the
black box and took out a folded paper. He held it firmly by one
corner as he turned and went hastily back to his place in the
crowd, where he stood a little apart from his family, not looking down at his hand.

"Allen," Mr. Summers said. "Anderson. . . . Bentham."

"Seems like there's no time at all between lotteries any
more," Mrs. Delacroix said to Mrs. Graves in the back row.
"Seems like we got through the last one only last week."

"Time sure goes fast," Mrs. Graves said.

"Clark. . . . Delacroix."

"There goes my old man," Mrs. Delacroix said. She held her
breath while her husband went forward.

"Dunbar," Mr. Summers said, and Mrs. Dunbar went
steadily to the box while one of the woman said, "Go on,
Janey," and another said, "There she goes."

"We're next," Mrs. Graves said. She watched while Mr.
Graves came around from the side of the box, greeted Mr.
Summers gravely, and selected a slip of paper from the box. By
now, all through the crowd there were men holding the small
folded papers in their large hands, turning them over and over
nervously. Mrs. Dunbar and her two sons stood together, Mrs.
Dunbar holding the slip of paper.

"Harburt. . . . Hutchinson."

"Get up there, Bill," Mrs. Hutchinson said, and the people
near her laughed.

"Jones."

"They do say," Mr. Adams said to Old Man Warner, who
stood next to him, "that over in the north village they're talking of giving up the lottery."

Old Man Warner snorted. "Pack of crazy fools," he said. "Listening to the young folks, nothing's good enough for *them*. Next thing you know, they'll be wanting to go back to living in caves, nobody work any more, live *that* way for a while. Used to be a saying about 'Lottery in June, corn be heavy soon.' First thing you know, we'd all be eating stewed chickweed and acorns. There's *always* been a lottery," he added petulantly. "Bad enough to see young Joe Summers up there joking with everybody."

"Some places have already quit lotteries," Mrs. Adams said.

"Nothing but trouble in that," Old Man Warner said stoutly. "Pack of young fools."

"Martin." And Bobby Martin watched his father go forward. "Overdyke. . . . Percy."

"I wish they'd hurry," Mrs. Dunbar said to her older son. "I wish they'd hurry."

"They're almost through," her son said.

"You get ready to run tell Dad," Mrs. Dunbar said.

Mr. Summers called his own name and then stepped forward precisely and selected a slip from the box. Then he called, "Warner."

"Seventy-seventh year I been in the lottery," Old Man Warner said as he went through the crowd. "Seventy-seventh time."

"Watson." The tall boy came awkwardly through the crowd. Someone said, "Don't be nervous, Jack," and Mr. Summers said, "Take your time, son."

"Zanini."

After that, there was a long pause, a breathless pause, until Mr. Summers, holding his slip of paper in the air, said, "All right, fellows." For a minute, no one moved, and then all the slips of paper were opened. Suddenly, all the women began to speak at once, saying, "Who is it?" "Who's got it?" "Is it the Dunbars?" "Is it the Watsons?" Then the voices began to say, "It's Hutchinson. It's Bill," "Bill Hutchinson's got it."

"Go tell your father," Mrs. Dunbar said to her older son.

People began to look around to see the Hutchinsons. Bill Hutchinson was standing quiet, staring down at the paper in his hand. Suddenly, Tessie Hutchinson shouted to Mr. Summers, "You didn't give him time enough to take any paper he wanted. I saw you. It wasn't fair!"

"Be a good sport, Tessie," Mrs. Delacroix called, and Mrs. Graves said, "All of us took the same chance."

"Shut up, Tessie," Bill Hutchinson said.

245 "Well, everyone," Mr. Summers said, "that was done pretty fast, and now we've got to be hurrying a little more to get done in time." He consulted his next list. "Bill," he said, "you draw for the Hutchinson family. You got any other households in the Hutchinsons?"

250 "There's Don and Eva," Mrs. Hutchinson yelled. "Make *them* take their chance!"

"Daughters draw with their husbands' families, Tessie," Mr. Summers said gently. "You know that as well as anyone else."

"It wasn't *fair*," Tessie said.

255 "I guess not, Joe," Bill Hutchinson said regretfully. "My daughter draws with her husband's family, that's only fair. And I've got no other family except the kids."

"Then, as far as drawing for families is concerned, it's you," Mr. Summers said in explanation, "and as far as drawing for 260 households is concerned, that's you, too. Right?"

"Right," Bill Hutchinson said.

"How many kids, Bill?" Mr. Summers asked formally.

"Three," Bill Hutchinson said. "There's Bill, Jr., and Nancy, and little Dave. And Tessie and me."

265 "All right, then," Mr. Summers said. "Harry, you got their tickets back?"

Mr. Graves nodded and held up the slips of paper. "Put them in the box, then," Mr. Summers directed. "Take Bill's and put it in."

270 "I think we ought to start over," Mrs. Hutchinson said, as quietly as she could. "I tell you it wasn't *fair*. You didn't give him time enough to choose. *Every*body saw that."

Mr. Graves had selected the five slips and put them in the box, and he dropped all the papers but those onto the ground, 275 where the breeze caught them and lifted off.

"Listen, everybody," Mrs. Hutchinson was saying to the people around her.

"Ready, Bill?" Mr. Summers asked, and Bill Hutchinson, with one quick glance around at his wife and his children, nodded.

280 "Remember," Mr. Summers said, "take the slips and keep them folded until each person has taken one. Harry, you help little Dave." Mr. Graves took the hand of the little boy, who came willingly with him up to the box. "Take a paper out of

the box, Davy," Mr. Summers said. Davy put his hand into the box and laughed. "Take just *one* paper," Mr. Summers said. "Harry, you hold it for him." Mr. Graves took the child's hand and removed the folded paper from the tight fist and held it while little Dave stood next to him and looked up at him wonderingly.

"Nancy next," Mr. Summers said. Nancy was twelve, and her school friends breathed heavily as she went forward, switching her skirt, and took a slip daintily from the box. "Bill, Jr.," Mr. Summers said, and Billy, his face red and his feet over-large, nearly knocked the box over as he got a paper out. "Tessie," Mr. Summers said. She hesitated for a minute, looking around defiantly, and then set her lips and went up to the box. She snatched a paper out and held it behind her.

"Bill," Mr. Summers said, and Bill Hutchinson reached into the box and felt around, bringing his hand out at last with the slip of paper in it.

The crowd was quiet. A girl whispered, "I hope it's not Nancy," and the sound of the whisper reached the edges of the crowd.

"It's not the way it used to be," Old Man Warner said clearly. "People ain't the way they used to be."

"All right," Mr. Summers said. "Open the papers. Harry, you open little Dave's."

Mr. Graves opened the slip of paper and there was a general sigh through the crowd as he held it up and everyone could see that it was blank. Nancy and Bill, Jr., opened theirs at the same time, and both beamed and laughed, turning around to the crowd and holding their slips of paper above their heads.

"Tessie," Mr. Summers said. There was a pause, and then Mr. Summers looked at Bill Hutchinson, and Bill unfolded his paper and showed it. It was blank.

"It's Tessie," Mr. Summers said, and his voice was hushed. "Show us her paper, Bill."

Bill Hutchinson went over to his wife and forced the slip of paper out of her hand. It had a black spot on it, the black spot Mr. Summers had made the night before with the heavy pencil in the coal-company office. Bill Hutchinson held it up, and there was a stir in the crowd.

"All right, folks," Mr. Summers said. "Let's finish quickly."

325     Although the villagers had forgotten the ritual and lost the original black box, they still remembered to use stones. The pile of stones the boys had made earlier was ready; there were stones on the ground with the blowing scraps of paper that had come out of the box. Mrs. Delacroix selected a stone so

330     large that she had to pick it up with both hands and turned to Mrs. Dunbar. "Come on," she said. "Hurry up."

    Mrs. Dunbar had small stones in both hands, and she said, gasping for breath, "I can't run at all. You'll have to go ahead and I'll catch up with you."

335     The children had stones already, and someone gave little Davy Hutchinson a few pebbles.

    Tessie Hutchinson was in the center of a cleared space by now, and she held her hands out desperately as the villagers moved in on her. "It isn't fair," she said. A stone hit her on the

340     side of the head.

    Old Man Warner was saying, "Come on, come on, everyone." Steve Adams was in the front of the crowd of villagers, with Mrs. Graves beside him.

    "It isn't fair, it isn't right," Mrs. Hutchinson screamed, and

345     then they were upon her.

[1948]

# Understanding the Story

1. Were you surprised by the ending? When did you finally realize what was going to happen? Looking back over the story, what hints of what is to come—what foreshadowing—can you find? For example, what details in the first three paragraphs create a picture of a peaceful rural village and what details don't fit that picture? (This unexpected contrast between the setting and action of a story is an example of dramatic irony.)

2. Over the years, how has the lottery changed? What aspects of it have remained the same? What saying

about the lottery does Old Man Warner remember? What connection does that rhyme suggest with the rituals of primitive cultures?

3. As the lottery was conducted, Mr. Summers spoke "soberly" (line 134) while Old Man Warner spoke "petulantly" (line 207). What difference does this show between the two men? What contrasting points of view on civic activities do they represent?

4. In each of the following sentences, what is the contrast between what the speaker means and what the reader understands? (These are good examples of verbal irony.)

   a. Chips of wood, Mr. Summers had argued, had been all very well when the village was tiny, but now that the population was more than three hundred . . . . (lines 75–77)

   In the 1940s in the U.S., a community of three hundred people was still considered very small. Why might it seem relatively large to Mr. Summers?

   b. "Bad enough to see young Joe Summers up there joking with everybody." (lines 208–9)

   Mr. Summers is probably in his fifties; would most people consider that "young"? Why might Old Man Warner see him that way?

   c. "People ain't the way they used to be." (line 305)

   What changes does Old Man Warner disapprove of? Do you think Old Man Warner himself is the way he used to be?

   d. "Be a good sport, Tessie." (line 242)

   In this context, what is the irony of urging someone to be "a good sport"?

5. What makes Tessie Hutchinson stand out from her neighbors when she first arrives (lines 110–17)? When does she first object to the lottery proceedings?

6. What builds tension in the final round of the drawing? Looking back over the story, how has the tension been built from the beginning?

7. What explanations can you suggest for the following contradictions in attitude:

   a. The townspeople felt sorry for Mr. Summers, we are told (lines 43–44), "because he had no children and his wife was a scold." Yet no one feels sorry for the annual victim of the lottery.

   b. Many parents say that they would gladly give their lives for their children. Yet Tessie wants her married daughter and the daughter's family to share the danger of being chosen.

   c. Nancy's friends hope that she will not be chosen. Yet they evidently don't mind that one member of Nancy's immediate family will be killed.

   d. In a small town, everyone speaks of close-knit families and good neighbors. Yet Tessie's husband and children, as well as her friends, participate in stoning her to death.

8. After Tessie has been identified as the victim, jovial Mr. Summers says (line 324), "All right, folks. Let's finish quickly." What is the dramatic irony of such a pleasant man encouraging a death by stoning? What is the verbal irony, considering their names, of Steve Adams and Mrs. Graves being at the front of the crowd?

## **D**eveloping a Way with Words

Some of the names in the story are those of people in North Bennington (e.g., Percy, from the family name Percey). However, many names have a more general significance. Some (e.g., Adams and Eva) are easy to recognize. For others (e.g., Tessie) you may need to consult a special dictionary of biography, or family names, or saints' names.

(All three kinds of dictionaries can be found in any good English-language library.)

1. How many of the following names can you find an association for?

   **Graves**—As an adjective, "grave" means serious. What does it mean as a noun?

   **Summers**—What seasonal association does this name have? The name is really derived from an occupation—*summoner*. What did the English summoners summon people to do? (A dictionary of names will provide the information.)

   **Warner**—If a summoner summons, what does a warner do?

   **Adams and Eva**—What Old Testament characters have similar names?

   **Little Dave/Davy**—What Old Testament character also threw small stones?

   **Delacroix**—What does this mean in French? What association does that have?

   **Harry Jones**—What does *harry* mean as a verb? Who is "the old Harry"? What does the sailors' term "Davy Jones' locker" refer to?

   **Hutchinson**—In Colonial American history, who was Anne Hutchinson?

   **Tessie (nickname for Teresa or Theresa)**—Who was St. Theresa of Avila? Who was Thérèse Martin (St. Thérèse of Liseux)?

2. For a writing project, discuss three or four of the names in terms of their origin and their significance in the story.

# aking Connections

1. How is the outcome of the lottery in this story different from the outcome of the lottery that Mr. Hattori wins in

"The Brown House"? Do you see any similarities between the two stories?

2. Before the lottery began, the men talked about "planting and rain, tractors and taxes" (line 27) and the women exchanged greetings and gossip.

   a. Why do you suppose no one mentioned what was going to happen?

   b. Do you think that most people avoid discussing something that they fear?

   c. What similarity is there to the situation in "The Chaser" by John Collier?

3. Jackson was frequently invited to read "The Lottery" and discuss it with college audiences. On those occasions, she read excerpts from the letters of puzzled or angry readers. She also told her audiences, "People at first [after the story appeared in *The New Yorker*] were not so much concerned with what the story meant; what they wanted to know was where these lotteries were held, and whether they could go there and watch." What connection, if any, can you see between that reaction and the view of human nature presented in "The Lottery"?

4. What other rituals—social, familial, religious—can you think of that are followed even though people no longer remember their origins? (Shaking hands and having a Christmas tree with lights are two examples.) What are other ways that people hold onto the past?

5. For a writing project, either use the library or interview elderly people in your community (or both) to investigate the origins of one or more rituals that you have taken for granted.

   a. How did the ritual begin?

   b. How has it changed over years?

   c. What purpose does the ritual serve that has kept it alive, even though people have forgotten its origin?

6. Can you think of examples of other activities that, like the lottery in this story, benefit some people while hurting others? Would you willingly participate in such an activity? What examples do you know—from history or current events or personal experience—of one person (or group of people) being forced to accept the blame—being used as "scapegoats"—for either a natural disaster or something done by others?

7. Many different interpretations have been offered for the story. Jackson (who, like most authors, didn't like to be asked to explain her work), gave at least four different responses to questioners: (1) she told a former teacher that the story was based entirely on his folklore course; (2) she accepted the interpretation of *The New Yorker's* publisher that the story was meant as an ironic contrast between an ancient superstition and a modern setting; (3) she told one friend that it was a picture of real people in North Bennington; and (4) she told another friend that it was a comment on anti-Semitism, derived from an unpleasant incident with a local shopkeeper. Others have suggested that the story is about choosing a scapegoat to assume the symbolic guilt for all of the sins of a community. Judy Oppenheimer, Jackson's biographer, describes "The Lottery" as "the purest, most direct expression [Jackson] would ever give to that knowledge of human evil she had carried within her since childhood."

When that many different explanations are possible, it's obvious that there can't be one "right" interpretation, though an explanation is certainly wrong if it contradicts the evidence of the story.

a. What is your interpretation of the story?

b. What reasoning and evidence have you used to arrive at that interpretation?

# A Blizzard Under Blue Sky

"When everything

in your life is

uncertain, there's

nothing quite like

the clarity and

precision of fresh

snow and blue

sky."

# A Blizzard Under Blue Sky

*Pam Houston*
*(born 1962)*

Pam Houston has taught creative writing at Denison University in Ohio, where she completed her undergraduate studies, and her short stories have appeared in various literary magazines. Presently completing her doctoral studies at the University of Utah, Houston is also part of the world of women's fashion magazines as a contributing editor for *Elle* and a frequent contributor to *Mirabella* and *Mademoiselle.* For a number of years, Houston has also worked part-time as a river guide and hunting guide in the western United States and has written about those activities for the publications *Outside* and *Travel and Leisure.*

Houston's interest in the outdoors forms the core of the stories in *Cowboys Are My Weakness* (1992), stories that have been described as "exhilarating, like a swift ride through river rapids," as well as "beautifully written and funny." In "A Blizzard Under Blue Sky," the exhilaration comes from sharing a winter adventure in the foothills of the Rocky Mountains, while the beauty of the writing is exemplified by this magical description of snow: "[it] stopped being simply white and became translucent, hinting at other colors, reflections of purples and blues and grays." Much of the humor in the story is based on the American fondness for believing that pets think and act like humans. Another feature of Houston's style is that she reflects her generation's habit of referring to items by brand names. She also sometimes teases by not directly identifying a character's gender, using a name that could be either a man's or a woman's and letting a simple pronoun do the work, perhaps contradicting the reader's expectations.

A heavy snowstorm with high winds, the "blizzard" of the title, matches the narrator's mood at the beginning of the story. She tells us that "everyone in Park City," a resort area near Salt Lake City, Utah, was happy except her. Could that be literally true, or is she exaggerating to make fun of herself? What could have caused such self-pity and depression? And what do you suppose she did about it? How did she find the "blue sky" that is the proverbial symbol of happiness?

## Uncommon Words or Meanings

**clinically depressed** ("The doctor said I was *clinically depressed.*")—suffering from a severe and continuing feeling of deep sadness.

**to run rampant** ("the month in which depression *runs rampant*")—to grow without limit.

**an inversion** ("the *inversion*-cloaked Salt Lake Valley")—an increase in air temperature with elevation that traps particles of dust and smoke at lower altitudes.

**an ex** ("weekending in the desert with his *ex*")—(informal) a previous romantic partner.

**a housemate** ("my *housemate,* Alex")—someone who shares the living space in a house.

**a bivvy sack** ("take my *bivvy sack*")—a large canvas bag.

**Kool-Aid** ("mix *Kool-Aid* with your water")—a brand of sugar and flavoring to be mixed with water to make a drink.

**lighting paste** ("don't forget *lighting paste* for your stove")—a sticky, flammable substance used to help wet wood burn.

**a butt** ("you are going to freeze your *butt*")—(informal) buttocks, the fleshy part of the body that one sits on.

**yin and yang** ("my *yin and yang* of dogs")—(Chinese philosophy) **yin,** the negative element, represents the female qualities of darkness and the sky; **yang,** the positive element, represents the male qualities of light and the earth.

**a Thermarest** ("My sleeping bag, my *Thermarest,* my stove")—a brand of inflatable, insulated mattress.

A Blizzard Under Blue Sky   

**Mountain House** ("*Mountain House* chicken stew")—a brand of freeze-dried food, eaten after boiling water is added.

**Carnation instant breakfast** ("*Carnation instant breakfast* for morning")—a brand of powered milk with flavoring and nutrients added, drunk after being mixed with water.

**Miles to go** ("*Miles to go,* Mom.")—an **allusion** (an indirect reference) to the closing lines of the poem "Stopping by Woods on a Snowy Evening" by Robert Frost: "But I have promises to keep, / And miles to go before I sleep, / And miles to go before I sleep."

**the fourth dimension** ("swears that Utah is the center of the *fourth dimension*")—something beyond length, breadth, and thickness (height, width, and depth); usually taken to be time.

**bindings** ("the squeaking of my *bindings*")—the foot fastenings on a ski.

**a dog tag** (the jangle of *dog tags*")—a small metal disk attached to a dog's collar to identify the dog's owner.

**primal** ("the bass line and percussion of some *primal* song")—from the time of the first humans.

**Moby Dick** ("I thought of *Moby Dick,* you know, the whiteness of the whale")—in Herman Melville's 19th-century novel of the same name, a huge white whale pursued by Captain Ahab.

**a fatality** ("winter camping *fatalities*")—an accidental death.

**couch potato** ("not so with Hailey, the *couch potato*")—(slang) the sort of person who likes best to sit on a couch while watching TV and eating.

**a mummy bag** ("inside my *mummy bag*")—a sleeping bag that is wider at the head than at the foot.

**to chastise** ("I spent half the night *chastising* myself ")—to criticize severely.

**Wonder Woman** ("thinking I was *Wonder Woman*")—a comic book character with superhuman powers.

**the Iditarod** ("run the *Iditarod*")—the annual 1,200-mile Alaskan dog sled race from Anchorage to Nome.

**to kayak** ("*kayaked* to Antarctica")—to travel in a kayak, a light single-seat boat propelled with a double paddle.

# A Blizzard Under Blue Sky

The doctor said I was clinically depressed. It was February, the month in which depression runs rampant in the inversion-cloaked Salt Lake Valley and the city dwellers escape to Park City, where the snow is fresh and the sun is shining and

5   everybody is happy, except me. In truth, my life was on the verge of more spectacular and satisfying discoveries than I had ever imagined, but of course I couldn't see that far ahead. What I saw was work that wasn't getting done, bills that weren't getting paid, and a man I'd given my heart to week-

10   ending in the desert with his ex.

    The doctor said, "I can give you drugs."

    I said, "No way."

    She said, "The machine that drives you is broken. You need something to help you get it fixed."

15     I said, "Winter camping."

    She said, "Whatever floats your boat."

    One of the things I love the most about the natural world is the way it gives you what's good for you even if you don't know it at the time. I had never been winter camping before, at least

20   not in the high country, and the weekend I chose to try and fix my machine was the same weekend the air mass they called the Alaska Clipper showed up. It was thirty-two degrees below zero in town on the night I spent in my snow cave. I don't know how cold it was out on Beaver Creek. I had listened to the

25   weather forecast, and to the advice of my housemate, Alex, who was an experienced winter camper.

    "I don't know what you think you're going to prove by freezing to death," Alex said, "but if you've got to go, take my bivvy sack; it's warmer than anything you have."

30     "Thanks." I said.

    "If you mix Kool-Aid with your water it won't freeze up," he said, "and don't forget lighting paste for your stove."

    "Okay," I said.

    "I hope it turns out to be worth it," he said, "because you

35   are going to freeze your butt."

    When everything in your life is uncertain, there's nothing quite like the clarity and precision of fresh snow and blue sky.

That was the first thought I had on Saturday morning as I stepped away from the warmth of my truck and let my skis slap the snow in front of me. There was no wind and no clouds that morning, just still air and cold sunshine. The hair in my nostrils froze almost immediately. When I took a deep breath, my lungs only filled up halfway.

I opened the tailgate to excited whines and whimpers. I never go skiing without Jackson and Hailey: my two best friends, my yin and yang of dogs. Some of you might know Jackson. He's the oversized sheepdog-and-something-else with the great big nose and the bark that will shatter glass. He gets out and about more than I do. People I've never seen before come by my house daily and call him by name. He's all grace, and he's tireless; he won't go skiing with me unless I let him lead. Hailey is not so graceful, and her body seems in constant indecision when she runs. When we ski she stays behind me, and on the downhills she tries to sneak rides on my skis.

The dogs ran circles in the chest-high snow while I inventoried my backpack one more time to make sure I had everything I needed. My sleeping bag, my Thermarest, my stove, Alex's bivvy sack, matches, lighting paste, flashlight, knife. I brought three pairs of long underwear—tops and bottoms—so I could change once before I went to bed, and once again in the morning, so I wouldn't get chilled by my own sweat. I brought paper and pen, and Kool-Aid to mix with my water. I brought Mountain House chicken stew and some freeze-dried green peas, some peanut butter and honey, lots of dried apricots, coffee and Carnation instant breakfast for morning.

Jackson stood very still while I adjusted his backpack. He carries the dog food and enough water for all of us. He takes himself very seriously when he's got his pack on. He won't step off the trail for any reason, not even to chase rabbits, and he gets nervous and angry if I do. That morning he was impatient with me. "Miles to go, Mom," he said over his shoulder. I snapped my boots into my skis and we were off.

There are not too many good things you can say about temperatures that dip past twenty below zero, except this: They turn the landscape into a crystal palace and they turn your vision into Superman's. In the cold thin morning air the trees and mountains, even the twigs and shadows, seemed to leap out of the background like a 3-D movie, only it was better than 3-D because I could feel the sharpness of the air.

80    I have a friend in Moab who swears that Utah is the center of the fourth dimension, and although I know he has in mind something much different and more complicated than subzero weather, it was there, on that ice-edged morning, that I felt on the verge of seeing something more than depth perception in
85    the brutal clarity of the morning sun.

As I kicked along the first couple of miles, I noticed the sun crawling higher in the sky and yet the day wasn't really warming, and I wondered if I should have brought another vest, another layer to put between me and the cold night ahead.

90    It was utterly quiet out there, and what minimal noise we made intruded on the morning like a brass band: the squeaking of my bindings, the slosh of the water in Jackson's pack, the whoosh of nylon, the jangle of dog tags. It was the bass line and percussion to some primal song, and I kept wanting to
95    sing to it, but I didn't know the words.

Jackson and I crested the top of a hill and stopped to wait for Hailey. The trail stretched out as far as we could see into the meadow below us and beyond, a double track and pole plants carving through softer trails of rabbit and deer.

100   "Nice place," I said to Jackson, and his tail thumped the snow underneath him without sound.

We stopped for lunch near something that looked like it could be a lake in its other life, or maybe just a womb-shaped meadow. I made peanut butter and honey sandwiches for all of
105   us, and we opened the apricots.

"It's fabulous here," I told the dogs. "But so far it's not working."

There had never been anything wrong with my life that a few good days in the wilderness wouldn't cure, but there I sat
110   in the middle of all those crystal-coated trees, all that diamond-studded sunshine, and I didn't feel any better. Apparently clinical depression was not like having a bad day, it wasn't even like having a lot of bad days, it was more like a house of mirrors, it was like being in a room full of one-way
115   glass.

"Come on, Mom," Jackson said. "Ski harder, go faster, climb higher."

Hailey turned her belly to the sun and groaned.

"He's right," I told her. "It's all we can do."

120 After lunch the sun had moved behind our backs, throwing a whole different light on the path ahead of us. The snow we moved through stopped being simply white and became translucent, hinting at other colors, reflections of blues and purples and grays. I thought of Moby Dick, you know, the 125 whiteness of the whale, where white is really the absence of all color, and whiteness equals truth, and Ahab's search is finally futile, as he finds nothing but his own reflection.

"Put your mind where your skis are," Jackson said, and we made considerably better time after that.

130 The sun was getting quite low in the sky when I asked Jackson if he thought we should stop to build the snow cave, and he said he'd look for the next good bank. About one hundred yards down the trail we found it, a gentle slope with eastern exposure that didn't look like it would cave in under any 135 circumstances. Jackson started to dig first.

Let me make one thing clear. I knew only slightly more about building snow caves than Jackson, having never built one, and all my knowledge coming from disaster tales of winter camping fatalities. I knew several things *not* to do when 140 building a snow cave, but I was having a hard time knowing what exactly to do. But Jackson helped, and Hailey supervised, and before too long we had a little cave built, just big enough for three. We ate dinner quite pleased with our accomplishments and set the bivvy sack up inside the cave just as the 145 sun slipped away and dusk came over Beaver Creek.

The temperature, which hadn't exactly soared during the day, dropped twenty degrees in as many minutes, and suddenly it didn't seem like such a great idea to change my long underwear. The original plan was to sleep with the dogs inside 150 the bivvy sack but outside the sleeping bag, which was okay with Jackson the super-metabolizer, but not so with Hailey, the couch potato. She whined and wriggled and managed to stuff her entire fat body down inside my mummy bag, and Jackson stretched out full-length on top.

155 One of the unfortunate things about winter camping is that it has to happen when the days are so short. Fourteen hours is a long time to lie in a snow cave under the most perfect of circumstances. And when it's thirty-two below, or forty, fourteen hours seems like weeks.

160　　　I wish I could tell you I dropped right off to sleep. In truth, fear crept into my spine with the cold and I never closed my eyes. Cuddled there, amid my dogs and water bottles, I spent half of the night chastising myself for thinking I was Wonder Woman, not only risking my own life but the lives of my dogs,
165　and other half trying to keep the numbness in my feet from crawling up to my knees. When I did doze off, I'd come back to my senses wondering if I had frozen to death, but the alternating pain and numbness that started in my extremities and worked its way into my bones convinced me I must still be alive.
170　　　It was a clear night, and every now and again I would poke my head out of its nest of down and nylon to watch the progress of the moon across the sky. There is no doubt that it was longest and most uncomfortable night of my life.

　　　But then the sky began to get gray, and then it began to get
175　pink, and before too long the sun was on my bivvy sack, not warm, exactly, but holding the promise of warmth later in the day. And I ate apricots and drank Kool-Aid-flavored coffee and celebrated the rebirth of my fingers and toes, and the survival of many more important parts of my body. I sang "Rocky
180　Mountain High" and "If I Had a Hammer," and yodeled and whistled, and even danced the two-stop with Jackson and let him lick my face. And when Hailey finally emerged from the sleeping bag a full hour after I did, we shared a peanut butter and honey sandwich and she said nothing ever tasted so good.

185　　　We broke camp and packed up and kicked in the snow cave with something resembling glee.

　　　I was five miles down the trail before I realized what had happened. Not once in that fourteen-hour night did I think about deadlines, or bills, or the man in the desert. For the first
190　time in many months I was happy to see a day beginning. The morning sunshine was like a present from the gods. What really happened, of course, is that I remembered about joy.

　　　I know that one night out at thirty-two below doesn't sound like much to those of you who have climbed Everest or
195　run the Iditarod or kayaked to Antarctica, and I won't try to convince you that my life was like the movies where depression goes away in one weekend, and all of life's problems vanish with a moment's clear sight. The simple truth of the matter is this: On Sunday I had a glimpse outside of the house of mir-
200　rors, on Saturday I couldn't have seen my way out of a paper bag. And while I was skiing back toward the truck that morning,

a wind came up behind us and swirled the snow around our bodies like a blizzard under blue sky. And I was struck by the simple perfection of the snowflakes, and startled by the hope-
*205* fulness of sun on frozen trees.

[1992]

## Understanding the Story

1. As the story opens, the narrator had been feeling extremely sad without a major reason ("clinically depressed," line 1) for a number of weeks.

   a. What two possible causes of depression does the narrator mention?

   b. Why do you think the narrator refused drugs as a cure? What did she decide to try instead?

   c. What did the doctor mean by her comment "Whatever floats your boat" (line 16)?

2. Immediately after describing her depression, the narrator says, "my life was on the verge of a more spectacular and satisfying discovery than I had ever imagined" (lines 5–7).

   a. What does it mean to "be on the verge of" a discovery?

   b. Why do you think the author chose to announce at the beginning that the story would turn out well? From the tone of the first few sentences, had you thought that the story might be an unhappy one? Why or why not?

3. What are some of the items the narrator planned to take on her overnight camping trip? What was the purpose of each item?

4. What makes Jackson and Hailey good friends to go camping with? What do you think the narrator means by calling them her "yin and yang of dogs" (line 46)?

5. How do the following comments and actions reflect the personality of each of the dogs?

   a. "Miles to go, Mom," [Jackson] said over his shoulder. (line 71)

   b. Hailey turned her belly to the sun and groaned. (line 118)

   c. "Put your mind where your skis are," Jackson said. (line 128)

   d. [Hailey and I] shared a peanut butter and honey sandwich and she said nothing ever tasted so good. (lines 183–84)

6. What specific details help the reader to imagine what it feels like to sleep outdoors in a snow cave when the temperature is forty degrees below zero?

7. How did the narrator's feelings change as a result of the winter camping experience? How is the story's title related to the change?

## D eveloping a Way with Words

1. Examine the paragraph that begins (line 90) "It was utterly quiet out there . . . ."

   a. What noises do the visitors from the city introduce?

   b. What does it mean to say (line 91) that these sounds "intruded on the morning like a brass band"? (This simile—a direct comparison—is also an example of hyperbole—a deliberate exaggeration.)

   c. What does the narrator mean by her musical metaphor (an implied comparison) in the statement (lines 93–95), "It was the bass line and percussion to some primal song, and I kept wanting to sing to it, but I didn't know the words."

2. In lines 111–15, the narrator uses a simile to explain how clinical depression feels.

a. What is the simile? Read it aloud.

b. What do you understand it to mean?

c. How does the narrator return to this simile in the final paragraph of the story?

# Making Connections

1. Reviewers have described Pam Houston's women as "strong and free-spirited" and "lean and tough, self-created adventurers." How well do those descriptions fit the narrator of this story? Houston has also been praised for the humor of her writing. What are some of the humorous parts of this story?

2. Find the full poem "Stopping by Woods on a Snowy Evening" by Robert Frost. (It appears in Frost's collected poems as well as in many anthologies.) Then discuss the following questions about the poem and the story.

   a. Some readers see the woods, which are "lovely, dark, and deep," and the idea of "sleep" as symbolic of death. Others argue for a more literal interpretation of the woods and sleep as representing a break in a busy life. What arguments can you think of to support each point of view?

   b. How does the horse make the poem's speaker remember his or her obligations to others?

   c. How is the quotation from the poem appropriate to Houston's story? For example, what obligations to others does the narrator of the story have?

3. Have you ever been deeply depressed? What was the cause? What did you do about it?

   (This might be a good question to answer in a ten-minute free writing that no one else will read.)

4. Have you ever gone winter camping? If so, what sort of preparations did you make and where did you sleep? If you are not a camper, do you think you'd like to try it one day? Why or why not?

5.  Have you ever had a sports adventure? If so, what details can you remember to help someone else to share your sense of the adventure?

6.  As a small library research project, look for newspaper or magazine accounts either of the Iditarod dog sled race (it began in 1974) or of attempts to climb Mount Everest (the first men to reach the summit were Sir Edmund Hillary and Tenzing Norgay in 1953). To organize the report, begin by presenting a question about the topic that you can answer in two or three pages.

# The Sentinel

"... it was that haunting doubt that had driven me forward. Well, it was a doubt no longer, but the haunting had scarcely begun."

# The Sentinel

*Arthur C. Clarke*
*(born 1917)*

Known for his ability to explain scientific ideas clearly and accurately to a popular audience, Arthur C. Clarke is even more famous as a master of science fiction whose work has been translated into more than thirty languages. He was born during the First World War in an English seaside town and fell in love with science fiction as a boy. When he left school at the age of sixteen and took a civil service job, reading and writing science fiction remained his hobby. Then, in what he has described as "probably the most decisive act of my entire life," Clarke gave up his safe job to enlist in the British Royal Air Force at the beginning of World War II. While training to be a radar instructor, he taught himself mathematics and electronic theory and continued writing.

Clarke is unique as a science fiction writer, for he has not only dreamed of what could be but has specified how it could be done. In 1945, for example, he explained how a satellite could be placed in synchronous orbit to receive and retransmit radio signals; eighteen years later, when the communications satellite became a reality, Clarke was honored for conceiving the idea. After the war, he earned a college degree in physics and pure and applied mathematics and became an editor for a technical journal. Soon, however, the success of his books *The Exploration of Space* (1952) and *Childhood's End* (1953) enabled Clarke to give up the editing job to concentrate on his own writing. While primarily known for his science fiction works, Clarke has also written on underwater diving (an interest that led him to build a home on the Indian Ocean) and scientific mysteries.

Clarke's fiction often deals with themes of exploration and discovery, always firmly grounded in scientific possibility. For example, in "The Sentinel," published in 1951, a party of scientists exploring the moon have chosen the same landing site as that used eighteen years later by real-life American astronauts. Clarke makes readers feel the wonder of scientific inquiry as the narrator describes an unexpected discovery, but Clarke also enables readers to recognize their own reality with details such as breakfast sausages.

In the early 1960s, Clarke became a Hollywood screen writer when film director Stanley Kubrick asked him to collaborate on a science fiction movie. The script, which was four years in development, drew in part on "The Sentinel," the pyramidal structure turning into a black monolith. The result, which has been called "the most important science fiction film ever made," was *2001: A Space Odyssey.* This film about the voyage of the spaceship *Discovery,* under the control of the computer HAL 9000, appeared in 1968. The next year, the American astronaut Neil Armstrong took what he called "one small step for man, one giant leap for mankind" when he left the ladder of his spacecraft to set foot on the moon's powdery surface. Except that the powder proved to be thicker than Clarke had imagined and that there is no moisture to produce hoarfrost, the moon's surface is much as described it in "The Sentinel." Yes, this story is by an Englishman who now lives in Sri Lanka. But as the songwriter Paul Simon says in "American Tune," the United States is "the ship that sailed the moon." And until someone else plants their flag there, we're going to claim the story.

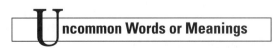

## Uncommon Words or Meanings

**a sentinel** (title)—a sentry, someone or something that stands guard.

**two o'clock** ("Round about *two o'clock* you will notice")—(military) the position where the two would be, if a clock face were superimposed on what you are looking at.

**a caterpillar tractor** ("our powerful *caterpillar tractors*")—a tractor with toothed wheels covered by a circular belt; used for heavy work on soft or uneven surfaces.

**pedantic** ("a geologist—or selenologist, if you want to be *pedantic*")—showing off academic knowledge.

**a flank** ("down the *flanks* of those stupendous cliffs")—the side of a mountain.

**to sit tight** ("radio for help and *sit tight*")—(informal) be patient and wait for the next event.

**a score** ("a *score* of rivers")—twenty.

**homely** ("so normal and *homely*")—(British usage) home-like.

**a galley** ("the corner . . . that served as a *galley*")—the kitchen on a ship or airplane.

**a log** ("entries in yesterday's *log*")—a book used on a ship or airplane for keeping a permanent daily record of events.

**degenerate** ("primitive plants and their slightly less *degenerate* ancestors")—(biology) having lost the normal or more highly developed characteristics of its type.

**a laughingstock** ("you'll be the *laughingstock* of the expedition")—a person or thing that is laughed at or made fun of.

**a [wild] goose chase** ("the craziest *goose chase* he had ever embarked on")—(idiom) a foolish or hopeless search (for something or somebody that can never be found).

**a folly** ("probably be called Wilson's *Folly*")—something foolish or ridiculous; here an allusion (an indirect reference) to "Seward's Folly," the mocking name given to the territory of Alaska in 1867, when Secretary of State Seward "wasted" $7,200,000 buying it from the Russian czar.

**haunting** ("*haunting* doubts had driven me forward")—returning to the mind repeatedly.

**to score** ("falling meteors had pitted and *scored*")—to mark with cuts, scratches, or lines.

**to ebb** ("as the life of the Moon *ebbed* with the dying oceans")—to become weak or faint.

**to crawl** ("set the scalp *crawling*")—to feel as though the flesh is covered with ants or another crawling thing.

**an atomic pile** ("an unshielded *atomic pile*")—the early name for a nuclear reactor.

**an apparition** ("crystalline *apparition*")—something strange that makes you doubt what you see.

**banked** ("those *banked* clouds of stars")—heaped up into a flat-topped mass.

# The Sentinel

The next time you see the full moon high in the south, look carefully at its right-hand edge and let your eye travel upward along the curve of the disk. Round about two o'clock you will notice a small, dark oval: anyone with normal eyesight can find
5  it quite easily. It is the great walled plain, one of the finest on the Moon, know as the Mare Crisium—the Sea of Crises. Three hundred miles in diameter, and almost completely surrounded by a ring of magnificent mountains, it had never been explored until we entered it in the late summer of 1996.
10  Our expedition was a large one. We had two heavy freighters which had flown our supplies and equipment from the main lunar base in the Mare Serenitatis, five hundred miles away. There were also three small rockets which were intended for short-range transport over regions which our sur-
15  face vehicles couldn't cross. Luckily, most of the Mare Crisium is very flat. There are none of the great crevasses so common and so dangerous elsewhere, and very few craters or mountains of any size. As far as we could tell, our powerful caterpillar tractors would have no difficulty in taking us wherever we
20  wished to go.
 I was geologist—or selenologist, if you want to be pedantic—in charge of the group exploring the southern region of Mare. We had crossed a hundred miles of it in a week, skirting the foothills of the mountains along the shore of what was
25  once the ancient sea, some thousand million years before. When life was beginning on Earth, it was already dying here. The waters were retreating down the flanks of those stupendous cliffs, retreating into the empty heart of the Moon. Over the land which we were crossing, the tideless ocean had once
30  been half a mile deep, and now the only trace of moisture was the hoarfrost one could sometimes find in caves which the searing sunlight never penetrated.
 We had begun our journey early in the slow lunar dawn, and still had almost a week of Earth-time before nightfall. Half
35  a dozen times a day we would leave our vehicle and go outside in the space suits to hunt for interesting minerals, or to place

markers for the guidance of future travelers. It was an uneventful routine. There is nothing hazardous or even particularly exciting about lunar exploration. We could live comfortably for a month in our pressurized tractors, and if we ran into trouble, we could always radio for help and sit tight until one of the spaceships came to our rescue.

I said just now that there was nothing exciting about lunar exploration, but of course that isn't true. One could never grow tired of those incredible mountains, so much more rugged than the gentle hills of Earth. We never knew, as we rounded the capes and promontories of that vanished sea, what new splendors would be revealed to us. The whole southern curve of the Mare Crisium is a vast delta where a score of rivers once found their way into the ocean, fed perhaps by the torrential rains that must have lashed the mountains in the brief volcanic age when the Moon was young. Each of these ancient valleys was an invitation, challenging us to climb into the unknown uplands beyond. But we had a hundred miles still to cover, and could only look longingly at the heights which others must scale.

We kept Earth-time aboard the tractor, and precisely at 22:00 hours the final radio message would be sent out to Base and we would close down for the day. Outside, the rocks would still be burning beneath the almost vertical sun, but to us it would be night until we awoke again eight hours later. Then one of us would prepare breakfast, there would be a great buzzing of electric razors, and someone would switch on the shortwave radio from Earth. Indeed, when the smell of frying sausages began to fill the cabin, it was sometimes hard to believe that we were not back on our own world—everything was so normal and homely, apart from the feeling of decreased weight and the unnatural slowness with which objects fell.

It was my turn to prepare breakfast in the corner of the main cabin that served as a galley. I can remember that moment quite vividly after all these years, for the radio had just played one of my favorite melodies, the old Welsh air "David of the White Rock." Our driver was already outside in his space suit, inspecting our caterpillar treads. My assistant, Louis Garnett, was up forward in the control position, making some belated entries in yesterday's log.

As I stood by the frying pan, waiting, like any terrestrial housewife, for the sausages to brown, I let my gaze wander

idly over the mountain walls which covered the whole of the southern horizon, marching out of sight to east and west
80　below the curve of the Moon. They seemed only a mile or two from the tractor, but I knew that the nearest was twenty miles away. On the Moon, of course, there is no loss of detail with distance—none of that almost imperceptible haziness which softens and sometimes transfigures all far-off things on Earth.
85　　　　Those mountains were ten thousand feet high, and they climbed steeply out of the plain as if ages ago some subterranean eruption had smashed them skyward through the molten crust. The base of even the nearest was hidden from sight by the steeply curving surface of the plain, for the Moon
90　is a very little world, and from where I was standing the horizon was only two miles away.
　　　　I lifted my eyes toward the peaks which no man had ever climbed, the peaks which, before the coming of terrestrial life, had watched the retreating oceans sink sullenly into their
95　graves, taking with them the hope and the morning promise of a world. The sunlight was beating against those ramparts with a glare that hurt the eyes, yet only a little way above them the stars were shining steadily in a sky blacker than a winter midnight on Earth.
100　　　　I was turning away when my eye caught a metallic glitter high on the ridge of a great promontory thrusting out into the sea thirty miles to the west. It was a dimensionless point of light, as if a star had been clawed from the sky by one of those cruel peaks, and I imagined that some smooth rock surface
105　was catching the sunlight and heliographing it straight into my eyes. Such things were not uncommon. When the Moon is in her second quarter, observers on Earth can sometimes see the great ranges in the Oceanus Procellarum burning with a blue-white iridescence as the sunlight flashes from their slopes and
110　leaps again from world to world. But I was curious to know what kind of rock could be shining so brightly up there, and I climbed into the observation turret and swung our four-inch telescope round to the west.
　　　　I could see just enough to tantalize me. Clear and sharp in
115　the field of vision, the mountain peaks seemed only half a mile away, but whatever was catching the sunlight was still too small to be resolved. Yet it seemed to have an elusive symmetry, and the summit upon which it rested was curiously flat. I stared for a long time at that glittering enigma, straining my eyes into

*Arthur C. Clarke*

120    space, until presently a smell of burning from the galley told me that our breakfast sausages had made their quarter-million-mile journey in vain.

     All that morning we argued our way across the Mare Cri-sium while the western mountains reared higher in the sky.
125 Even when we were out prospecting in the space suits, the discussion would continue over the radio. It was absolutely certain, my companions argued, that there had never been any form of intelligent life on the Moon. The only living things that had ever existed there were a few primitive plants and their
130 slightly less degenerate ancestors. I knew that as well as anyone, but there are times when a scientist must not be afraid to make a fool of himself.

     "Listen," I said at last, "I'm going up there, if only for my own peace of mind. That mountain's less than twelve thousand
135 feet high—that's only two thousand under Earth gravity—and I can make the trip in twenty hours at the outside. I've always wanted to go up into those hills, anyway, and this gives me an excellent excuse."

     "If you don't break your neck," said Garnett, "you'll be the
140 laughingstock of the expedition when we get back to Base. That mountain will probably be called Wilson's Folly from now on."

     "I won't break my neck," I said firmly. "Who was the first man to climb Pico and Helicon?"

     "But weren't you rather younger in those days?" asked
145 Louis gently.

     "That," I said with great dignity, "is as good a reason as any for going."

     We went to bed early that night, after driving the tractor to within half a mile of the promontory. Garnett was coming
150 with me in the morning; he was a good climber, and had often been with me on such exploits before. Our driver was only too glad to be left in charge of the machine.

     At first sight, those cliffs seemed completely unscalable, but to anyone with a good head for heights, climbing is easy on
155 a world where all weights are only a sixth of their normal value. The real danger in lunar mountaineering lies in overconfidence; a six-hundred-foot drop on the Moon can kill you just as thoroughly as a hundred-foot fall on Earth.

     We made our first halt on a wide ledge about four thou-
160 sand feet above the plain. Climbing had not been very difficult, but my limbs were stiff with the unaccustomed effort, and I

was glad of the rest. We could still see the tractor as a tiny metal insect far down at the foot of the cliff, and we reported our progress to the driver before starting on the next ascent.

165   Inside our suits it was comfortably cool, for the refrigeration units were fighting the fierce sun and carrying away the body heat of our exertions. We seldom spoke to each other, except to pass climbing instructions and to discuss our best plan of ascent. I do not know what Garnett was thinking, prob-
170   ably that this was the craziest goose chase he had ever embarked upon. I more than half agreed with him, but the joy of climbing, the knowledge that no man had ever gone this way before, and the exhilaration of the steadily widening landscape gave me all the reward I needed.

175   I don't think I was particularly excited when I saw in front of us the wall of rock I had first inspected through the telescope from thirty miles away. It would level off about fifty feet above our heads, and there on the plateau would be the thing that had lured me over these barren wastes. It would be,
180   almost certainly, nothing more than a boulder splintered ages ago by a falling meteor, and with its cleavage planes still fresh and bright in this incorruptible, unchanging silence.

There were no handholds on the rock face, and we had to use a grapnel. My tired arms seemed to gain new strength as I
185   swung the three-pronged metal anchor round my head and sent it sailing up toward the stars. The first time it broke loose and came falling slowly back when we pulled the rope. On the third attempt, the prongs gripped firmly and our combined weights could not shift it.

190   Garnett looked at me anxiously. I could tell that he wanted to go first, but I smiled back at him through the glass of my helmet and shook my head. Slowly, taking my time, I began the final ascent.

Even with my space suit, I weighed only forty pounds
195   here, so I pulled myself up hand over hand without bothering to use my feet. At the rim I paused and waved to my companion, then I scrambled over the edge and stood upright, staring ahead of me.

You must understand that until this very moment I had
200   been almost completely convinced that there could be nothing strange or unusual for me to find here. Almost, but not quite; it was that haunting doubt that had driven me forward. Well, it was doubt no longer, but the haunting had scarcely begun.

I was standing on a plateau perhaps a hundred feet across.
It had once been smooth—too smooth to be natural—but
falling meteors had pitted and scored its surface through
immeasurable eons. It had been leveled to support a glittering,
roughly pyramidal structure, twice as high as a man, that was
set in the rock like a gigantic, many faceted jewel.

Probably no emotion at all filled my mind in those first
few seconds. Then I felt a great lifting of my heart, and a
strange, inexpressible joy. For I loved the Moon, and now I
knew that the creeping moss of Aristarchus and Eratosthenes
was not the only life she had brought forth in her youth. The
old, discredited dream of the first explorers was true. There
had, after all, been a lunar civilization—and I was the first to
find it. That I had come perhaps a hundred million years too
late did not distress me; it was enough to have come at all.

My mind was beginning to function normally, to analyze
and to ask questions. Was this a building, a shrine—or something for which my language had no name? If a building, then
why was it erected in so uniquely inaccessible a spot? I wondered it if might be a temple, and I could picture the adepts of
some strange priesthood calling on their gods to preserve
them as the life of the Moon ebbed with the dying oceans, and
calling on their gods in vain.

I took a dozen steps forward to examine the thing more
closely, but some sense of caution kept me from going too
near. I knew a little of archaeology, and tried to guess the cultural level of the civilization that must have smoothed this
mountain and raised the glittering mirror surfaces that still
dazzled my eyes.

The Egyptians could have done it, I thought, if their work-
men had possessed whatever strange materials these far more
ancient architects had used. Because of the thing's smallness,
it did not occur to me that I might be looking at the handiwork
of a race more advanced than my own. The idea that the Moon
had possessed intelligence at all was still almost too tremen-
dous to grasp, and my pride would not let me take the final,
humiliating plunge.

And then I noticed something that set the scalp crawling
at the back of my neck—something so trivial and so innocent
that many would never have noticed it at all. I have said that
the plateau was scarred by meteors; it was also coated inches
deep with the cosmic dust that is always filtering down upon

the surface of any world where there are no winds to disturb
it. Yet the dust and the meteor scratches ended quite abruptly
in a wide circle enclosing the little pyramid as though an invisible wall was protecting it from the ravages of time and the
250    slow but ceaseless bombardment from space.

        There was someone shouting in my earphones, and I
realized that Garnett had been calling me for some time. I
walked unsteadily to the edge of the cliff and signaled him to
join me, not trusting myself to speak. Then I went back
255    toward that circle in the dust. I picked up a fragment of splintered rock and tossed it gently toward the shining enigma. If
the pebble had vanished at that invisible barrier, I should not
have been surprised, but it seemed to hit a smooth, hemi-
spheric surface and slide gently to the ground.

260        I knew then that I was looking at nothing that could be
matched in the antiquity of my own race. This was not a building, but a machine, protecting itself with forces that had chal-
lenged Eternity. Those forces, whatever they might be, were
still operating, and perhaps I had already come too close. I
265    thought of all the radiations man had trapped and tamed in the
past century. For all I knew, I might be as irrevocably doomed
as if I had stepped into the deadly, silent aura of an unshielded
atomic pile.

        I remember turning then toward Garnett, who had joined
270    me and was now standing motionless at my side. He seemed
quite oblivious to me, so I did not disturb him but walked to the
edge of the cliff in an effort to marshal my thoughts. There
below me lay the Mare Crisium—Sea of Crises, indeed—
strange and weird to most men, but reassuringly familiar to me.
275    I lifted my eyes toward the crescent Earth, lying in her cradle
of stars, and I wondered what her clouds had covered when
these unknown builders had finished their work. Was it the
steaming jungle of the Carboniferous, the bleak shoreline over
which the first amphibians must crawl to conquer the land—or,
280    earlier still, the long loneliness before the coming of life?

        Do not ask me why I did not guess the truth sooner—the
truth that seems so obvious now. In the first excitement of my
discovery, I had assumed without question that this crystalline
apparition had been built by some race belonging to the
285    Moon's remote past, but suddenly, and with overwhelming
force, the belief came to me that it was as alien to the Moon as
I myself.

In twenty years we had found no trace of life but a few degenerate plants. No lunar civilization, whatever its doom, could have left but a single token of its existence.

I looked at the shining pyramid again, and the more I looked the more remote it seemed from anything that had to do with the Moon. And suddenly I felt myself shaking with a foolish, hysterical laughter, brought on by excitement and overexertion: for I had imagined that the little pyramid was speaking to me and was saying, "Sorry, I'm a stranger here myself."

It has taken us twenty years to crack that invisible shield and to reach the machine inside those crystal walls. What we could not understand, we broke at last with the savage might of atomic power and now I have seen the fragments of the lovely, glittering thing I found up there on the mountain.

They are meaningless. The mechanisms—if indeed they are mechanisms—of the pyramid belong to a technology that lies far beyond our horizon, perhaps to the technology of paraphysical forces.

The mystery haunts us all the more now that the other planets have been reached and we know that only Earth has ever been the home of intelligent life in our Universe. Nor could any lost civilization of our own world have built that machine, for the thickness of the meteoric dust on the plateau has enabled us to measure its age. It was set there upon its mountain before life had emerged from the seas of Earth.

When our world was half its present age, *something* from the stars swept through the Solar System, left this token of its passage, and went again upon its way. Until we destroyed it, that machine was still fulfilling the purpose of its builders; and as to that purpose, here is my guess.

Nearly a hundred thousand million stars are turning in the circle of the Milky Way, and long ago other races on the worlds of other suns must have scaled and passed the heights that we have reached. Think of such civilizations, far back in time against the fading afterglow of Creation, masters of a universe so young that life as yet had come only to a handful of worlds. Theirs would have been a loneliness we cannot imagine, the loneliness of gods looking out across infinity and finding none to share their thoughts.

They must have searched the star clusters as we have searched the planets. Everywhere there would be worlds, but

they would be empty or peopled with crawling, mindless
330    things. Such was our own Earth, the smoke of the great volca-
noes still staining the skies, when that first ship of the peoples
of the dawn came sliding in from the abyss beyond Pluto. It
passed the frozen outer worlds, knowing that life could play
no part in their destinies. It came to rest among the inner plan-
335    ets, warming themselves around the fire of the Sun and waiting for their stories to begin.

Those wanderers must have looked on Earth, circling
safely in the narrow zone between fire and ice, and must have
guessed that it was the favorite of the Sun's children. Here, in
340    the distant future, would be intelligence; but there were count-
less stars before them still, and they might never come this
way again.

So they left a sentinel, one of millions they scattered
throughout the Universe, watching over all worlds with the
345    promise of life. It was a beacon that down the ages patiently
signaled the fact that no one had discovered it.

Perhaps you understand now why that crystal pyramid
was set upon the Moon instead of on the Earth. Its builders
were not concerned with races still struggling up from sav-
350    agery. They would be interested in our civilization only if we
proved our fitness to survive—by crossing space and so escap-
ing from the Earth, our cradle. That is the challenge that all
intelligent races must meet, sooner or later. It is a double challenge, for it depends in turn upon the conquest of atomic
355    energy and the last choice between life and death.

Once we had passed that crisis, it was only a matter of
time before we found the pyramid and forced it open. Now its
signals have ceased, and those whose duty it is will be turning
their minds upon Earth. Perhaps they wish to help our infant
360    civilization. But they must be very, very old, and the old are
often insanely jealous of the young.

I can never look now at the Milky Way without wondering
from which of those banked clouds of stars the emissaries are
coming. If you will pardon so commonplace a simile, we have
365    set off the fire alarm and have nothing to do but to wait.

I do not think we will have to wait for long.

[1951]

# Understanding the Story

1. What is the span of time discussed in the story? According to the story, when did exploration on the moon begin? When is the story being told?

2. What specific facts does the reader learn about the narrator in the course of the story?

3. According to the story, what difficulties do scientists face in the lunar environment? How are these difficulties brought out in the story?

4. While Wilson is staring at a "glittering enigma" on the horizon (line 119), he is suddenly "brought back to earth" (to use an idiom not found in the story) by an occurrence much "closer to home" (another idiom). What is the occurrence?

5. Why did Wilson's companions say that Wilson would be the "laughingstock" (line 140) of the expedition if he went to investigate the reflected sunlight? How did they tease him about his idea of climbing the mountain?

6. When Wilson reached the plateau at the top of the cliff, what was his first analysis of what he found? What second discovery "set the scalp crawling at the back of [his] neck" (lines 241–42)?

7. Discuss what Wilson means by each of the following statements.

   a. . . . I had been almost completely convinced that there could be nothing strange or unusual for me to find here. Almost, but not quite; it was that haunting doubt that had driven me forward. (lines 199–202)

   "Almost, but not quite" what? What was the "haunting doubt"?

   b. For all I knew, I might be as irrevocably doomed as if I had stepped into the deadly, silent aura of an unshielded atomic pile. (lines 266–68)

If someone unknowingly came near an unshielded nuclear reactor, what sort of trouble would he or she be in? Why wouldn't the person be aware of the trouble?

c. . . . I had imagined that the little pyramid was speaking to me and was saying, "Sorry, I'm a stranger here myself." (line 296)

In what situation does someone normally make an apology like that?

d. What we could not understand, we broke at last with the savage might of atomic power . . . . (lines 298–300)

What does Wilson mean by "the savage might of atomic power"? How is it ironic (the opposite of what one might logically expect) to smash something that, after long effort, you still can't understand?

e. . . . long ago other races on the worlds of other suns must have scaled and passed the heights we have reached. (lines 319–21)

What "heights" is Wilson referring to? Who does he mean by "we"?

8. Discuss Wilson's ideas and theories about the machine at the time he is telling the story:

a. Why is he sure that it was not made by any beings in Earth's solar system, "our Universe" (line 308)?

b. Who does he think made it?

c. For what purpose does he think it was made?

9. Wilson feels that the machine's purpose has now been fulfilled.

a. What does he think will happen next?

b. Discuss the implications of his statement (lines 359–61), "Perhaps they wish to help our infant civilization. But they must be very, very old, and the old are often insanely jealous of the young."

c. Could it be said that Wilson and his companions are just "sitting tight," as Wilson once said they could always do if they ever "ran into trouble" (lines 40–41)?

## Developing a Way with Words

1. Like all good scientific writers, Clarke uses context to clarify the meaning of many words in this story. In the following sentences, how are the words in dark type explained by the rest of the sentence? Where else in the story can a reader use the context to understand the meaning of a word?

   a. one of my favorite melodies, the old Welsh **air** "David of the White Rock" (lines 71–72)

   b. a vast **delta** where a score of rivers once found their way into the ocean (lines 49–50)

   c. . . . those cliffs seemed completely **unscalable,** but to anyone with a good head for heights, climbing is easy on a world where all weights are only a sixth of their normal value. (lines 153–55)

   d. There were no handholds on the rock face, and we had to use a **grapnel.** My tired arms seemed to gain new strength as I swung the three-pronged metal anchor round my head and set it sailing up toward the stars. (lines 183–86)

2. Many scientific words are composed of Latin and Greek prefixes, suffixes, and roots, some of which are listed below. Use the information in the list to explain the words in dark type in the examples that follow it.

| Prefixes | Suffixes | Roots |
|---|---|---|
| *archaeo-* ancient times | *-escence* a continuing state | *helios* the sun |
| *geo-* the earth (Greek) | *-graph* an instrument that writes or records | *iris* a rainbow |
| *para-* beyond | | *selene* the moon |
| *physi(o)-* relating to nature or natural forces | *-ist* a specialist in | *terra* the earth (Latin) |
| | | *-ology* the study of |

a. I was **geologist**—or **selenologist,** if you want to be pedantic—in charge of the group exploring the southern region of Mare. (lines 21–23)

b. As I stood by the frying pan, waiting, like any **terrestrial** housewife, for the sausages to brown . . . . (lines 76–77)

c. . . . some smooth rock surface was catching the sunlight and **heliographing** it straight into my eyes (lines 104–6)

d. . . . the great ranges in the Oceanus Procellarum burning with a blue-white **iridescence** (lines 107–9)

e. I knew a little of **archaeology,** and tried to guess the cultural level of the civilization that must have smoothed this mountain . . . . (lines 229–31)

f. The mechanisms . . . of the pyramid belong to a technology that lies far beyond our horizon, perhaps to the technology of **paraphysical** forces. (lines 302–5)

3. As a writer, Clarke has been praised not only for his scientific imagination but also for his poetry. Explain the similes (direct comparisons) and metaphors (implied comparisons) in dark type in the following sentences. What other similes and metaphors did you notice in the story?

a. **as if a star had been clawed from the sky** by one of those **cruel** peaks (lines 103–4)

b. see the tractor **as a tiny metal insect** far down at the **foot** of the cliff (lines 162–63)

c. sent it **sailing** up toward the stars (line 186)

d. the crescent Earth, **lying in her cradle of stars** (lines 275–76)

## M aking Connections

1. How realistic do you find the characters in this story? What nationality would you say they are? Do they match your idea of scientists and space explorers? Why or why not?

2. Human beings, as a race, have a need to explore the unknown. What do you think explains that need? Would you like to be part of a scientific expedition to outer space? Why or why not?

3. In the story, written in 1951, humans have established and staffed a scientific base for long-term exploration on the moon by the year 1996. Why do you think that hasn't happened?

4. What major scientific advances have been made in your parents' lifetimes? What advances have you been aware of so far in your lifetime? What further advances do you hope to live to see?

5. When the next full moon comes, go outdoors one evening to look for the Mare Crisium—the Sea of Crises. Alternatively, find a map of the moon in an atlas. On the "near" side, find the geographical features—the Mare Crisium, the Mare Serenitatis, the Oceanus Procellarum (the Ocean of Storms), and the craters Aristarchus and Eratosthenes—mentioned in the story.

6. Arrange to see the film *2001: A Space Odyssey.* (It is available on video cassette.) Then discuss how the film differs from this story. Alternatively, read and discuss the novel *2001: A Space Odyssey,* which Clarke wrote while the film was being made.

# Text Credits

"No Speak English": From THE HOUSE ON MANGO STREET. Copyright © 1989 by Sandra Cisneros. Published in the United States by Vintage Books, a division of Random House, Inc., New York, and distributed in Canada by Random House of Canada Limited, Toronto. Originally published, in somewhat different form, by Arte Publico Press in 1984 and revised in 1989. Reprinted by permission of Susan Bergholz Literary Services, New York.

"Popular Mechanics": Reprinted by permission of Tess Gallagher. Copyright © 1978 by Tess Gallagher.

"The Unicorn in the Garden": From FABLES FOR OUR TIME by James Thurber (Hamish Hamilton, 1939) copyright © James Thurber, 1939, copyright © Helen Thurber, 1968. Reproduced by permission of Hamish Hamilton Ltd.

"The Summer of the Beautiful White Horse": From MY NAME IS ARAM by William Saroyan. Copyright © 1938 and renewed 1966 by William Saroyan. Reprinted by permission of Harcourt Brace & Company. Acknowledgement to The William Saroyan Foundation.

"Samuel": From ENORMOUS CHANGES AT THE LAST MINUTE by Grace Paley. Copyright © 1968, 1974 by Grace Paley. Reprinted by permission of Farrar, Straus & Giroux, Inc.

"The Chaser": Copyright © 1940, 1967 by John Collier. Reprinted by permission of Harold Matson Company, Inc.

"The Brown House": From SEVENTEEN SYLLABLES AND OTHER STORIES by Hisaye Yamamoto. Copyright © 1988 by Hisaye Yamamoto. Used by permission of the author and of Kitchen Table: Women of Color Press, P. O. Box 908, Latham, N.Y. 12110 on all reprinted materials.

"Love": From DAWN OF REMEMBERED SPRINGS by Jesse Stuart. Copyright © 1940 by Jesse Stuart. Copyright © renewed 1968 by Jesse Stuart Foundation. Reprinted by permission of Jesse Stuart Foundation, P. O. Box 391, Ashland, Kentucky, 41114.

Quotes on Pages 84–85 used by permission of the Jesse Stuart Foundation, Box 391, Ashland, Kentucky 41114.

## Art Credit